The Apostolic
Of Hippolytus
Translated Into English With Introduction And Notes

Antipope Hippolytus, Burton Scott Easton

Alpha Editions

This Edition Published in 2021

ISBN: 9789355399786

Design and Setting By
Alpha Editions
www.alphaedis.com
Email – info@alphaedis.com

#

TABLE OF CONTENTS

#

INTRODUCTION

I. CHURCH ORDERS

The early Church Orders were systematic manuals of disciplinary and liturgical rules for which the collective authority of the whole apostolate was claimed. They made their appearance in the second century, grew to considerable dimensions in the third, and reached their fullest development toward the end of the fourth century. They are sources of importance for our knowledge of the inner life of the church, and they were influential factors in the formation of the later canon law.

That legislation of a fairly detailed and elaborate character should sooner or later make its appearance in Christianity was inevitable. The local congregations were made up of men and women practically isolated from the rest of the world and brought into the closest contact with one another; their church was to them almost their entire universe. If human beings anywhere are to live together under such conditions, mutual affection and forbearance—be they never so great—are not enough. Regulations, which define rights and duties in unambiguous terms, are indispensable, and these regulations are bound to increase in number and complexity as the community grows.

As it happened, however, Christianity in its origins contained extraordinarily little material that could be used in forming these regulations. In theory Christians, for guidance in all matters, were to turn to Jesus Christ their Lord, whose teaching they regarded as totally divine and so the final authority in all things. But, as a matter of fact, Jesus' concern was not with concrete and specific problems, and when asked to rule on such he brusquely refused.[1] He occupied himself with ultimate moral principles, and left to individuals the task of applying these principles to the various special problems of their lives. Hence it is not at all surprising that in the apostolic and post-apostolic ages direct citation of his sayings is rarely used to settle disputed matters of practice;[2] his words are employed rather as general directives and to give inspiration to action.[3]

Nor did the apostles attempt in any systematic way to supply the concrete element that Jesus' teaching might be thought to lack. In only one instance[4] does the New Testament give us anything that purports to be an apostolic decree, and it gives this only in a matter of fundamental importance. Yet even this brief ruling presents serious critical difficulties to modern investigators, and probably something less than full apostolic authority should be accorded it. In St Paul's Epistles, indeed, it is laid down as a fundamental principle that individual divergences should be tolerated as far as possible even in the same community,[5] so that the apostle turns from general principles to detailed regulations only in the most extreme instances. Each of his churches was left free to develop under the guidance of the Spirit such customs as it might judge profitable—and was warned not to make even these customs too authoritative. And there is no reason to think that the other apostles differed greatly from St Paul in this regard. That some of them may have drawn up certain specific rules for their own communities is abstractly conceivable, but as to this there is no tradition at all in the sources of the apostolic age and nothing of any value in later writings.

As a consequence, Christian congregations in search for material to use for legislative purposes could find very little in the primary authoritative teaching of their religion, and were obliged to look elsewhere. But abundant other sources were not lacking.

Of these the chief was the Old Testament, whose importance to the majority of early Christians can hardly be exaggerated. The ceremonial legislation of the Pentateuch was, to be sure, no longer regarded as binding on Christians; the Pauline controversies had settled this principle, even though a dissenting minority did not disappear until late in the second century. But acceptance of the principle did not debar endless debate as to the principle's precise extent: just what Mosaic precepts should be classed as "purely ceremonial"? St Paul, for instance, saw no inherent objection to eating things sacrificed to idols,[6] but in the decree of Acts 15. 28-29 abstinence from such food is regarded as axiomatically "necessary",[7] and Christians during the next three centuries generally took the same view. The duty of Christian liberality was defined more closely by the adoption of the Jewish law of tithing, and this law was even extended to include not only agricultural produce but income of any kind.[8] Or, even when the literal force of an Old Testament precept was recognized as superseded, a transferred sense might be discovered that revived the rule for Christianity. So the command that tithes should be paid to the priests was construed to give the church's ministers a right to the

Christian payments.[9] Or the fact that the Old Testament ministry was strictly regulated led to the argument that divine regulations of equal strictness must hedge about the Christian ministry as well.[10]

Since so much permanent value was detected in the older ceremonial legislation, it was only natural that the obligation of the "moral" laws should usually be treated as absolute. This led to a true moral legalism; that is, these laws were conceived to demand obedience not because of a higher principle contained in them but simply because they were "written". Such, for instance, is the assumption throughout Clement's letter to the Corinthians, where almost every argument is made to rest ultimately on an Old Testament precept. Nor does it occur at all to Clement that the Corinthians may find anything amiss in his method; he takes for granted that, no matter how much other parts of the Old Testament may have lost their meaning, God's moral statutes will remain in immutable force for ever. And, we can scarcely doubt, such was a common opinion in Christianity from the very beginning, outside of Pauline and a few other circles; it was an attitude very like Clement's that St Paul combated in his Epistle to the Romans.

This common opinion, moreover, was strongly reinforced by pedagogical needs. The sweep of the new religion and its gathering in converts from all sorts of curious moral highways and hedges had created a situation that taxed to the uttermost the powers of the Christian teachers. Multitudes of neophytes were constantly demanding instruction, and to teach each one of them how to apply Christ's deeper principles to involved special problems seemed utterly impracticable; why engage in so intricate a task when a succinct Old Testament precept could settle the matter instantly? So catechetical moral training was usually given by means of short digests based on Old Testament laws, some of these digests being undoubtedly of Jewish origin.[11] But it is interesting to note that the most authoritative brief digest of Jewish morality—the Decalogue—does not appear as a whole in the Christian teaching.[12]

In Gentile Christianity concrete rules were taken likewise from Greek ethical works, whose standard was usually high. Only the learned, of course, could appreciate the moral treatises of the great philosophers, but a long succession of teachers—chiefly Stoics—had devoted themselves to bringing an understanding of good conduct within the reach of all. Among other means, these teachers achieved their purpose by requiring their pupils to memorize short gnomic formulas, or—the ultimate extremity of simplification—bare lists of virtues to be imitated or vices to be avoided.[13] This last device was so convenient that even Greek-speaking Jews adopted it,[14] and Christians found it invaluable. In fact they did not hesitate to take ready-made lists from Stoic and other sources,[15] so giving Greek ethical concepts an unnoticed but authoritative entrance into Christianity.

Less formal but very real was the influence of established customs and conventions—on occasion, even superstitions—in contemporary life, whether Jewish or Gentile. St Paul, for instance, in 1 Corinthians 11. 4 holds it to be obvious that men should pray with their heads uncovered, and this passage has influenced all subsequent Christian practice. Yet the ruling rests on nothing more profound than the religious habits of the particular Jews among whom St Paul was brought up; other Jews in his day believed that God should be approached only when the head was covered, and this came to be the accepted Jewish practice. If St Paul had lived elsewhere—or if he had been born somewhat later—the declaration in 1 Corinthians 11. 4 would have shocked him.

To these customs inherited from their pre-conversion days, the various local churches gradually added customs of their own. Some of these were certainly introduced for very good reasons, others perhaps for no particular reason and more or less accidentally. But in religious bodies everywhere customs quickly grow to be revered simply because they *are* the custom, and are clung to tenaciously. Yet, to a certain degree, the churches were willing to learn from one another. The Christian communities in any geographical subdivision of the Empire had strong interests in common, and, in particular, they recognized as right and proper a certain leadership on the part of the church in their political capital. So the customs of this church were generally accepted as models for the whole region, with the result that by the end of the second century "local" use was quite generally converted into "provincial" use. And very large and important churches—especially Antioch, Alexandria and Rome—gained a corresponding ascendency over the smaller capitals within their respective areas.

In some instances, in fact, rulings by outstanding churches or individuals might acquire an almost world-wide influence. 1 Clement, which states the Roman conception of certain rules governing the ministry, was accepted as authoritative in circles far away from the Corinthians for whom it was written. Indeed, many Christians came actually to regard it as an inspired New Testament writing, and in various later documents Clement figures as the medium through whom the apostles issued their decrees. Of equal significance was Ignatius of Antioch, whose directions on church organization appear to have been obeyed even in Rome itself. Just so later Church Orders were regarded as legally binding in provinces remote from their place of origin.

In most quarters this trend toward uniformity in the second century was simply taken for granted. Practices with a century of tradition[16] behind them were practically treated as irreformable: "This custom has been handed down from the days of the apostles and consequently has the apostles' authority behind it". But even by the end of the first century the apostles were regarded as a wholly inspired group, who were the divinely appointed custodians and interpreters of the faith.[17] Hence, it was commonly assumed, they must have been unanimous in all things; what one apostle taught all apostles must have taught. All Christianity rests on a common norm of doctrine and practice that was delivered to the church by the apostles.[18]

It is this conviction that lies behind the Church Orders and that gives them their peculiar form.

The most obvious objection to this theory, naturally, was the very evident fact that approved practices in different localities varied considerably; these could not all go back to a common origin. And in minor matters, assuredly, second- and third-century Christianity tolerated or even encouraged[19] differences. But in anything regarded as important local divergences could lead to bitter conflict. When the second-century Asia Minor churches were asked to change their date for Easter, they replied, "We must obey God rather than men", and a schism in the church resulted.[20] And in this clash apostolic authority was passionately claimed by both sides, with the constant premise that such authority must in the main lead to uniformity.

Yet there were definite limits to the process of unification. As the generations grew into centuries, the general "ethos" of the more important local types of Christianity acquired a venerable dignity that commanded respect even from churches whose customs were different. In major matters of practice, moreover, a substantial agreement had been achieved, and the churches were organized along the same main lines everywhere. So when any church claimed apostolic teaching in support of special usages of its own—and such claims were made frequently—it usually did so fully aware that other churches could make similar claims with equal validity, and that its special usages might very well have been different. This fact led to a revision of the theory of apostolic unanimity. The complete agreement of the apostles was now thought to extend only to doctrine and the vitally important rules of practice; in other regards each apostle within his own territory had established a use of his own—and each of these uses was equally legitimate. So Alexandria appealed to St Mark, Jerusalem to St James, Ephesus to St John, Rome to St Peter, and so on; in due course the far east was to appeal to St Thomas or St Thaddeus.

Such a theory was not entirely novel; Irenaeus, for instance, urged it in an unsuccessful attempt to settle the paschal controversy. But as local customs became fixed the theory was more and more invoked, and it finally became a settled principle throughout Christendom. The fourth century was here the definite turning point; when the ecumenical councils met, they made no attempt to legislate in full details for the whole church. So when the compiler of the Apostolic Constitutions *ca.* 375 revived the Church Order formula that made all the apostles legislate minutely, we may presume that he was consciously adopting a style that was already somewhat obsolescent; Christians by now were becoming aware that collective apostolic authority could not be claimed for so wide an extent of regulations. And this consciousness brought with it the eventual end of the Church Orders; they were replaced by explicitly local collections of canons and by liturgical service books. Yet in many parts of the church the old Church Orders retained their authority, and they were incorporated into the manuals of canon law.

The following are the chief Church Orders:

THE DIDACHE

As this work is familiar to everyone its contents need not be described. Most scholars date it in the early years of the second century, but the possibility that its compiler used the Epistle of Barnabas as a source cannot be wholly disregarded.[21] Barnabas is usually dated about 131, with a possibility of belonging some fifteen years earlier, so if the dependence is accepted the Didache could scarcely have originated before the second quarter of the century and may even be somewhat later.

The influence of the Didache in the early church was wide and it was held in high honour. It was incorporated into the Didascalia, the Apostolic Church Order and the Apostolic Constitutions. So eminent and orthodox a saint as Athanasius speaks of it as a book very profitable for neophytes "who wish for instruction in the word of godliness",[22] and he cites it as an authority more than once, even though he—very properly—refuses to recognize it as a canonical New Testament writing.[23] There consequently can be no reasonable doubt that the Didache originated in the broad stream of orthodox Christian tradition, not in some obscure heretical sect.

Much the most convenient edition of the Greek text is that edited by Dr Hans Lietzmann in his *Kleine Texte* series;[24] it contains an excellent critical apparatus and is very inexpensive. There are many accessible English translations.

THE APOSTOLIC TRADITION

This work of Hippolytus, the subject of the present volume, is named here to preserve the chronological sequence. In its Coptic and other versions it was formerly known as the Egyptian Church Order.

THE DIDASCALIA

A substantial "handbook for the churches", written probably in Syria, not far either way from 250. Its original language was Greek, but it has been preserved in Syriac and Latin; the latter is defective. It is concerned almost wholly with rules for church organization, church finance and church discipline, treating doctrine hardly at all and liturgical matters only incidentally. Its author was acquainted with the more important Christian literature of the second century, and there is some evidence that he knew Hippolytus's Apostolic Tradition.

The Didascalia is best studied in Dom R. H. Connolly's English version,[25] which he has provided with judicious introduction and notes. Attention should be directed to his words on p. xlv: "It is now generally recognized that the author's theological outlook was entirely Catholic, and that he writes as a champion of the Great Church as opposed to all manner of heresy and schism".

THE APOSTOLIC CHURCH ORDER

This work[26] so nearly resembles the Didache in both size and arrangement that there is good reason to believe that it was originally issued as a "revised" edition of the older work. Chapters 1-3 describe a meeting of the Twelve Apostles at which they decided to publish this Order. Chapters 4-13 are Didache 1-4, slightly rearranged and expanded. Chapter 14 is apparently derived from Barnabas 14 and closes with Didache 4. 13. Chapters 15-28 treat of church organization, beginning with the election of bishops and ending with the duties of women: the conditions described indicate a date not earlier than the end of the third century. Chapter 29 contains an adjuration to charity and chapter 30 a final appeal to apostolic authority.

This Order, whose orthodoxy is unimpeachable, was written in Greek and is probably (not certainly) of Egyptian origin. Its popularity is shown by the fact that Latin, Syriac, Sahidic, Bohairic, Ethiopic and other versions have been preserved, as well as the original Greek. A complete critical edition has not yet been prepared. The best edition of the Greek text is in Theodor Schermann's *Die allgemeine Kirchenordnung*,[27] 1, pp. 1-34. The English versions, such as they are, are not very accessible, but the translations of the Ethiopic, Arabic and Sahidic in Horner are adequate.[28]

THE APOSTOLIC CONSTITUTIONS

This, the most ambitious of all the Church Orders, undertook to provide a practically complete treatise on church law and liturgics by collecting and revising earlier authoritative sources. Books I-VI are an enlarged edition of the Didascalia. Chapters 1-32 of Book VII treat the Didache similarly; chapters 33-45 contain a collection of prayers obviously based on Jewish synagogue forms; the source of chapters 46-49 is uncertain. Chapters 1-2 of Book VIII are now generally held to utilize a lost work of Hippolytus, *Concerning Gifts*. Chapters 3-46 contain his Apostolic Tradition, greatly expanded, especially in the so-called Clementine Liturgy[29] of chapters 6-15.

The Constitutions were compiled around 375, either in Syria or Constantinople. The author had no hesitation about drastically rewriting archaic material, but the great bulk of his expansions are simply expository and homiletic. His verbosity is irksome to modern readers, but it was quite in accord with the taste of his age. Theologically he shows Arian leanings, but these are often rather difficult to detect without comparing his text with its sources; his work as a whole is certainly not "Arian".

The extent of the later influence of the Constitutions has not yet been satisfactorily estimated. That the work in its entirety was not apostolic was recognized at once and various church councils branded it as apocryphal. But later writers not infrequently cite passages from the Constitutions as authoritative; these citations as a whole, however, have not thus far been collected and analysed. Apparently the most influential part of the book was its "Clementine Liturgy", which deeply influenced subsequent Eastern rites.

The classic edition of the Greek text is that of Funk. The English translation in the *Ante-Nicene Fathers* is generally adequate.

THE APOSTOLIC CANONS

A collection of eighty-five canons, appended to the Constitutions. They were compiled by its author partly from earlier synodic sources, partly from the Constitutions themselves. In the Eastern Church these canons were accepted as a whole and were translated into many languages; in the Western Church only the first fifty were received.

THE EPITOME

"The Epitome of the Eighth Book of the Apostolic Constitutions" is the title—and something of a misnomer—for what is little more than a copy of the sections of this Book of the Constitutions that deal with organization and discipline. It is divided into five parts, A-E. The first two chapters of the Constitutions are reproduced in A, chapter 32 in C, chapter 46 in E. D contains chapters 33-34, 42-45, practically intact.

B is headed "The Constitutions of the Holy Apostles concerning Ordination through Hippolytus", a title not infrequently[30] used to describe the entire work as "The Constitutions through Hippolytus". It begins with chapter 3 of the Constitutions, describing the election of a bishop. But the ordination prayer that follows is taken directly from Hippolytus's Apostolic Tradition, not from the Constitutions. Then comes chapter 16 of the Constitutions on the ordination of presbyters. The opening sentences are given literally, but the ordination prayer is about midway in length between the compact version in Hippolytus and the elaborate wording of the Constitutions. Chapters 18-21 are copied with minimal variations, but in chapter 22 the ordination of readers is dismissed in a brief sentence from Hippolytus. Chapters 23-28 and 30-31, almost unchanged, conclude the section.

Even as late as the beginning of the twentieth century the Epitome was often taken to be a source used in the Constitutions. But this is now recognized to be wrong: the Epitome is extracted from the Constitutions, with a few reversions to Hippolytus. As it contains nothing independent there is no way to judge its date or place of origin.

The Greek text will be found in Funk, II, pp. 72-96. The three passages that really differ from the Constitutions are translated in the present volume.[31]

THE TESTAMENT OF OUR LORD

This work is divided into two Books, of 47 and 27 chapters respectively. In Book I, after an apocalyptic introduction in chapters 1-13, the risen Christ solemnly declares (chapters 14-18) to the apostles the divine obligation of the rules that follow. The remainder of the work is based on Hippolytus's Apostolic Tradition, although often greatly changed and expanded: there are added, for instance, rules for church architecture, descriptions of clerical duties and much liturgical matter. But Hippolytus's order is faithfully followed and his text is often reproduced verbally. Book I, chapter 28, a "mystagogic" treatise on Christology in semi-credal form, is perhaps a later addition.

The date of the Testament is probably a little later than that of the Constitutions; in any case it is hardly earlier than 360. For its place of origin Syria, Asia Minor and Egypt all have their advocates, with Egypt probably the least likely. The original Greek is lost, but the work has been transmitted in Syriac, Ethiopic and Arabic. Its Christology has an "Apollinarian" flavour, but "there is no actual heresy in the Testament".[32] The English version of Cooper and Maclean is standard, although certain of their elaborate notes now require revision.

THE CANONS OF HIPPOLYTUS

A work containing thirty-eight "canons", which "Hippolytus, the chief of the bishops of Rome, wrote according to the commands of the apostles". This paraphrase for his "Apostolic Tradition" indicates the source with an explicitness unusual in a Church Order. Its alterations are much less radical than those in the Testament, and wholly new matter is limited to a brief introduction and an appendix concerned chiefly with moral and ascetic directions. The revision was made almost certainly in the fifth century and beyond reasonable doubt in Egypt.

The text (originally Greek) has been preserved only in an Arabic version. The only reliable edition is the German translation by Riedel; an English version is badly needed.

For the sake of completeness there may be added:

SARAPION'S PRAYERS

This work is not a true Church Order: it makes no pretence to apostolic origin and consists wholly of a collection of prayers drawn up by Sarapion, bishop of Thmuis, about 350. It opens with the celebrant's part at the eucharist and closes with various benedictions. The eucharistic prayer has been strongly influenced by the Didache, the ordination prayers by Hippolytus. The most accessible edition of the Greek text is in Funk, II, pp. 158-195. Bishop John Wordsworth edited an excellent English translation.

II. HIPPOLYTUS

Hippolytus is a unique figure in Christian history, for he, a schismatic bishop of Rome, is honoured by the Roman church as a saint and martyr. This curious combination of qualities made him for centuries a highly enigmatic personality, of whom almost nothing was known. Many of his voluminous works were preserved and studied, and were translated into Syriac, Coptic, Arabic, Armenian and even Old Slavic. But his creation of a schism and his acceptance of its episcopate were acts so contrary to established principles that Eusebius, writing less than a century later, can describe him only as the bishop "of a church somewhere";[33] to which description Jerome adds: "the name of whose city I have been unable to learn".[34] That this city was in fact Rome is, to be sure, stated by not a few late patristic and medieval writers, especially in the East, but these do not hint that there was anything irregular about his tenure. Or he is assigned sees in widely different localities, sometimes as far off as Arabia and sometimes as near Rome as Portus: this last place—due, apparently, to confusion with some other martyr—was especially popular. But among Western writers Hippolytus's episcopal rank is commonly ignored and he appears simply as "a presbyter": the present Roman Catholic service books[35] do not call him "bishop". The sole general agreement was as to the date of his death, which the martyrologies and other early testimony place about 235.

In 1551 excavations in Rome brought to light a third-century statue of Hippolytus, now in the Lateran Museum; the upper part of the body has been "restored". On the sides are inscribed an "Easter Canon" that he computed and a partial list of his works.[36] The posture of the body, which is that of a seated teacher, made episcopal dignity more than probable, so for the official description of the statue Pius IV, the next pope, adopted the Portus tradition. Hence as "Bishop of Portus" the saint was generally known until the middle of the nineteenth century.

In 1701 Jakob Gronov published, in the tenth volume of his *Thesaurus Graecarum Antiquitatum*, Book I—no more was then known—of a work called "Philosophumena" or "Philosophizings", that was commonly, although not universally, referred to Origen. Books IV-X of this work were discovered in 1842 and nine years later were published as Origen's by the editor, B. E. Miller.[37] But the contents of the work were soon proved by competent scholars—notably Döllinger[38]—to make Origen's authorship impossible; the necessary conditions were fulfilled by Hippolytus alone. This proof established also the Hippolytean authorship of certain other disputed works; and the evidence thus assembled showed that Hippolytus was both a bishop and a Roman. Incidentally, it has been established also that the correct title for the above work is "Refutation of All Heresies", and that "Philosophumena" was the sub-title of Books I-IV (not as is sometimes stated of Book I alone). But "Philosophumena" is generally accepted by modern writers.

The Portus tradition, however, still lingered on for a time and is accepted in the *Ante-Nicene Fathers*, both by the original editor J. H. Macmahon (1868) and by the American reviser Bishop A. C. Coxe (1886). Bishop Lightfoot supported a compromise theory that made of Hippolytus a sort of suffragan bishop of Rome with special jurisdiction over Portus.[39] But neither position is now tenable.

For the facts of Hippolytus's life we have practically only what he himself tells us in scattered allusions; only once (Philosophumena IX, 7) does he relate contemporary events at any length. Since in his later works he speaks of himself as aged, his birth must be placed *ca.* 160. Tradition makes him a disciple of Irenaeus, a highly probable supposition even though his works are silent on the subject. He became a presbyter of the Roman church under Zephyrinus (198?-217, or perhaps earlier) and won great respect for his learning and eloquence: on one occasion he was deputed to preach in the presence of Origen.[40] But his learning brought him into a mortal conflict with a fellow presbyter, one Callistus.

This Callistus had had in earlier years a career that was at least ambiguous. The servant of a wealthy Christian, he was permitted by his master to undertake in Rome the experiment of a "Christian bank", in which many of the faithful deposited their savings. As has usually been the case with such experiments, the bank failed, and in this case no assets could be discovered. Callistus fled, but was brought back to Rome and sentenced to the treadmill. After a while he was released and sought to regain favour with the Christians by interrupting a Jewish synagogue service and preaching Christianity to the congregation.[41] For this he was sent to the Sardinian convict mines. All of this appears to have taken place during the ninth decade of the second century; in any case Callistus was still a prisoner when Bishop Victor succeeded in obtaining from the Emperor Commodus the release of many Christian prisoners in the year 190 or thereabouts.[42] The list of names drawn up by Victor and sent to Sardinia did not include Callistus, but he contrived to secure his discharge as well, and he returned to Italy as at least technically a "martyr".[43] Victor, however, did not permit him to remain in Rome and dismissed him to Antium, where he lived until Victor's death, receiving from the church's fund a monthly allowance that enabled him to avoid suffering.

Victor was succeeded by Zephyrinus, an easy-going man of small intelligence, who in past years had conceived an intense admiration for Callistus. He immediately recalled the latter to Rome, ordained him presbyter,[44] and made him his chief lieutenant; during Zephyrinus's episcopacy Callistus was the real power at Rome. His only significant rival was Hippolytus.

Two more different men can scarcely be imagined. Both were equally determined to have their own way. But Callistus was suave and ingratiating, little concerned with theological speculation, desirous of immediate practical results and none too scrupulous as to ways and means, indifferent to precedents and perfectly willing to try novel experiments. Hippolytus was dour and irascible,[45] convinced that meticulous theology must be maintained though the heavens fell, scandalized at the mere thought of relaxing discipline, a traditionalist to his finger tips, who believed that any new idea was necessarily Satanic. Between such antagonists a relentless war was inevitable.

They appear to have fought on most questions, but one cause of conflict was paramount: Christology. During the second century the church was constantly tormented by the problem of reconciling the rigid monotheism inherited from the Jews with the divine honours that were unquestioningly paid to Christ. The solution that Hippolytus proposed followed in general the doctrine of the Fourth Gospel: God from before creation has begotten[46] from Himself His Logos, itself divine. This doctrine rests on speculative metaphysical premises that are none too easy of comprehension; to many thinkers in the second century it seemed either (*a*) to subordinate the Son to the Father in such a way as to detract from the Son's true divinity, or (*b*) to make of the Son an independent deity and so destroy monotheism. Hippolytus endeavoured to avoid both extremes, but with what success specialists—ancient or modern—are unable to agree; it must be remembered, however, that he wrote as a pioneer in an age when the real questions were not yet clearly stated, let alone answered, and that he employed a philosophy originally devised for a very different purpose. The most popular alternative to his theory was what is rather cumbrously known as "modalistic monarchianism"; this was quite within the grasp of the most unphilosophical, since it disregarded all metaphysical refinements. It argued: "We worship Christ as God, and God is One. Therefore Christ is God and God is Christ; 'Father' and 'Son' are only titles that describe the same Person in different aspects or 'modes'".

Later on this modalism was regarded as heresy of the most extreme type, but even in the late second century it was widely taught and was uncondemned; in part the church authorities wished to preserve peace above all things and in part they were really in doubt as to the points at issue. Many teachers, to be sure, attacked it violently and none with greater passion than Hippolytus, who at the beginning of the third century was making the Roman church hot with his invectives. But, despite him, when Sabellius, the great apostle of modalism, came to Rome he was received cordially by Zephyrinus and Callistus.

Still, even Hippolytus was forced to admit that Sabellius was an honest and open-minded man, and one with whom he could argue so frankly that he had great hopes of converting him. But Callistus interfered. Not that he himself was quite a modalist; his own Christology, while having strong modalistic leanings, was saved from downright modalism by dexterous qualifications. But he regarded Hippolytus's doctrine—which he probably could not really understand—as the worse of the two evils. So Sabellius, finding the two great Roman leaders at loggerheads, reverted to his former position. To Hippolytus this was the last straw and he publicly denounced Callistus[47] as a heretic. Callistus retorted by hurling at Hippolytus the final insult: "Ditheist!" The result was a schism.

It took place, apparently, in the last years of Zephyrinus,[48] who died in 217. Hippolytus and his disciples fled from the—to them—polluted and heretical communion of the regular bishop and proclaimed that they and they alone were the true church of Rome. They were not numerous but their standing appears to have been high; at any rate they were able to find bishops willing to consecrate their leader to the episcopate. But their withdrawal left the "regular" church completely under Callistus's control, and at Zephyrinus's death he was elected to succeed him. This election, of course, Hippolytus treated as wholly null, asserting contemptuously that what Callistus had done was to become the leader of a "school of Callistans", not of a "church of Christians".

Callistus disposed of the Christological controversy by excommunicating both Sabellius and Hippolytus, and then turned his attention to the most thorny practical question that perplexed contemporary Christians, the problem of mortal sin after baptism. From the beginning of the post-apostolic age[49] the church almost universally held that such sin could not receive absolution, so that the sinners were permanently excommunicate and without hope of restoration.[50] The only "orthodox" voice in opposition to this rigorism was raised by the Shepherd of Hermas, and even its author dared oppose the universal teaching of his age only because he had received a special revelation from God; nor did he venture to promise more than the remission of *one* post-baptismal sin for anyone. In many quarters, indeed, even this mild relaxation of the rule was passionately resisted, and the most vigorous religious movement of the second century—Montanism—took as its watchword, "No second remission!"

By the beginning of the third century a final settlement of the question had become a necessity. The Christians had been successful beyond their dreams in attracting converts, but probably the majority possessed only general good moral qualities and lacked the heroic virtues. What was to be done with them? Should the church dismiss them as unworthy and so reduce its numbers drastically? Or should it do what it could for those whose intentions were good, without expecting too much of them? To Hippolytus the church's constant teaching since the apostles' time removed the problem from debate: Christians must be saints in the fullest sense of the word. So his flock was constantly purged by excommunications. Callistus, on the contrary, took the bold step of brushing aside tradition altogether and of appealing directly to the New Testament: "Let the tares grow with the wheat until the harvest",[51] and, "Who art thou that judgest another man's servant?"[52] Sinners were, of course, put to penance, but if they proved their good faith they could be absolved, no matter what their offence nor how often it had been committed. This decision of Callistus was nothing short of revolutionary, and it was destined to change the ideal of church membership for all time. Naturally it shocked Hippolytus beyond measure—and his horror was intensified when those whom he himself had excommunicated were received into communion by Callistus.

The latter, in fact, went so far in the abolition of the stricter rules that his own successors at Rome withdrew or seriously modified some of his concessions. He pronounced that second and even third marriages constituted no impediment to ordination, and allowed clerics to marry after they had been ordained. And he declined to recognize for Christian marriage the impediment of disparity of status in the Roman civil law; as a result the church permitted marriages that the parties could disown to the state—with some curious consequences.

All of this so incensed Hippolytus and his party that Callistus's death in 222 did not end the schism; it continued under his successors Urbanus (222-230)—of whom nothing is certainly known—and Pontianus (230-235). But in 235 Maximinus became emperor and he undertook a persecution that singled out the Christian leaders. So in Rome both Pontianus and Hippolytus were arrested and sent to Sardinia, where they shortly afterward succumbed to the hardships of convict life. This healed the breach in the church, and the reunited factions completed the reconciliation by pronouncing both bishops to be saints and martyrs.

This action has been taken by some scholars—arguing from the premises of a later day—as evidence that Hippolytus made a retractation before his death. But Hippolytus was not the man to retract anything. And the Roman church of the next generation would never have allowed the erection of his statue if they had held him to be saved only by a deathbed repentance; still less would they have permitted the public and honourable inscription of the titles of works in which he glories in his conduct.[53] The church really acknowledged that both sides had made mistakes, and that Hippolytus's errors—whatever they may have been—

were due to an excess of zeal for righteousness and were not to be weighed against his consecrated learning and his burning devotion.

THE APOSTOLIC TRADITION

For a list and description of Hippolytus's works reference must be made to the treatises on patrology; he was a prolific writer on exegetical, doctrinal and practical themes, who published at least fifty books and probably many more. But after he had been consecrated bishop of his separatist congregation, his first task was to provide treatises to perpetuate the principles for which he was contending so bitterly. One of these was *Of Gifts*, to which he alludes in 1. 1; it has not been preserved, although traces appear to be incorporated in Constitutions VIII, i-ii. And it was followed immediately by the Apostolic Tradition.

Its introduction fixes its date and purpose. A "lapse or error" had "recently occurred" (1. 4), and Hippolytus undertakes to guard against its effects by setting forth the true doctrine "which has continued up to now". And he recurs to the same theme at the close: "the many heresies have increased because their leaders would not learn the purpose of the apostles", but "over all who hear the apostolic tradition and keep it, no heretics or any other man will prevail" (38. 2-3). The date accordingly must be close to 217 and the purpose is to cleave to the old ways, rejecting every innovation; the tradition which Hippolytus received from the presbyters before him (36. 12) must be maintained inviolate.

In content the book consists mainly of laws for church organization and the conduct of worship, but these are interspersed freely with comment and explanation. The source of the laws themselves is not doubtful: they represent the normal practices at Rome in Hippolytus's younger days, and he is quite sincere in believing that they are truly apostolic and therefore unalterable. And that they actually are rules of real antiquity is shown by the corroboration they receive from other early Christian writers, among whom Tertullian in particular describes usages extraordinarily like those expounded by his Roman contemporary. The Apostolic Tradition, consequently, is more than a source for Roman customs at the beginning of the third century; it may with equal safety be invoked for the practice of thirty or even fifty years earlier. In the words of Harnack:[54] "Here is the richest source that we in any form possess for our knowledge of the polity of the Roman church in the oldest time, and this Roman polity may, in many regards, be accepted as the polity held everywhere".

The same, naturally, cannot always be said of the material in Hippolytus's comments. Here too, unquestionably, much is inherited; it is for one of his explanations that he appeals to the presbyters in 36. 12. But it is occasionally evident—chapter 9 is an instance—that the ceremonies he faithfully describes do not fully accord with his interpretations, and that he himself does not invariably understand his material. Some of the wording of his prayers, moreover, is unmistakably his own, but in his day (10. 4-6) each Christian leader still felt free to frame prayers as he would.

Hippolytus designed his work for "the churches" (1. 3), a phrase most naturally understood of Christendom at large. His own church of Rome appears to have appreciated his work the least, for the majority of Roman Christians gave their allegiance to his rivals and accepted their legislation; it was the reforms of Callistus and not the conservatism of Hippolytus that directed subsequent Roman polity. Probably, too, despite his canonization, his memory was always slightly suspect; the Roman church certainly managed to forget very quickly who he really was. By the middle of the third century, moreover, his church finally abandoned Greek as its official language and became wholly Latinized, so that his writings were no longer accessible. And what was true of Rome was true of the West in general.

In the East, however, especially in Egypt and Syria, Hippolytus's work was accepted as possessing high authority. It was of course not treated as infallible, for later legal writers do not hesitate to amend or omit laws disagreeing with local usage. Yet the title Hippolytus chose for his work was taken really seriously,[55] and he, more than any other Church Father, gave the laws and the liturgy of the Eastern Church their permanent form.

The Apostolic Tradition was first made known to the Western world in 1691 by Job Ludolf in *Ad suam Historiam Aethiopicam Commentarius*; in this he published in incomplete form the Ethiopic work containing it, to which he gave the title—still in use—of *Statuta Apostolorum*. But he naturally was unable to identify the author. It was not until 1848 that the next contribution was made, Tattam's *The Apostolic Constitutions or Canons of the Apostles in Coptic*,[56] which gave the Bohairic text with an English translation. The Sahidic text appeared thirty-five years later on pp. 248-266 of Lagarde's *Aegyptiaca*, and this is still the standard edition. A German translation (by Steindorff) was published in 1891 by Achelis in his *Die ältesten Quellen des orientalischen Kirchenrechtes*:[57] this monograph opened the really critical study of the material and is not yet wholly obsolete. But Hauler's discovery of the Latin text was the most important event of all. He published his find in 1900 but did not appreciate the full importance of what he describes only as "Aegyptiorum reliquiae" at the end of his long title.[58] And even such an intensely able scholar as Funk, in making his own Latin version of "The Egyptian Church Order", still preferred to follow the Sahidic.[59] Horner's *Statutes of the Apostles* (1904) finally supplied critical Ethiopic and Arabic texts, with scientifically literal translations of these and of the Sahidic as well.

The basic significance of the Latin version was glimpsed by Cooper and Maclean in their edition of the Testament[60] (1902); their use of "Hauler" is often penetrating. In 1906 Baron Eduard von der Goltz[61] finally identified certain sections as definitely Hippolytean, and four years later Dr Eduard Schwartz reached the definite conclusion:[62] the Latin text represents substantially what Hippolytus wrote. Dr Schwartz's monograph, however, was brief and left many problems unexplored; the detailed demonstration was the—wholly independent—work of Dom Connolly in 1916.

In 1928 Dr Jungklaus published a German translation of Hippolytus's work, with an elaborate introduction; in some regards it proved unsatisfactory but it should on no account be neglected.

The textual evidence is as follows:

The original Greek of chapters 3 and 12 is preserved in the Epitome, and that of 25. 1-2 in the Vienna fragment printed (e.g.) by Funk (II, p. 112). The Constitutions also give some aid in reconstructing the Greek text elsewhere.

The Latin codex, now in Verona, is a palimpsest,[63] probably of the sixth century, over which some two centuries later three books of Isidore of Seville's *Sentences* were written. The translation itself appears to have been made in the fourth century, and is a rendition of a Greek book of church laws, in which Hippolytus's book is preceded by portions of the Didascalia and the complete Apostolic Church Order. The translator, who presumably had no idea of the authorship of the closing portion, made his version pedantically literal; a great advantage to the modern student. Unquestionably neither the sixth-century copyist, the translator nor the Greek text used was infallible; the last certainly contained duplications.[64] But the version is incomparably the best guide that we have. It includes 1. 1-9. 11a, 21. 14-24. 12a, 26. 3b-38. 2a.

The Oriental manuscripts, all comparatively modern,[65] are fairly numerous,[66] and are likewise collections of laws. The Sahidic—known also as the Egyptian Heptateuch, from its seven Books—begins with the Apostolic Church Order. Then (Book II) comes Hippolytus's work, in which chapters 1, 3, 4. 4-13, 5-6, 8. 2-5, 9. 9-12 are omitted and chapters 11-14 are arranged in the order[67] 12, 14, 11, 13; there are also minor variations to which attention is usually called in the translation and notes. Books III-VI are parallel to Constitutions VIII; Book VII contains the Apostolic Canons. Like other Coptic ecclesiastical writings it teems with transliterated Greek words, so that the original terms are obvious. But the first translator was evidently often in doubt as to the meaning of the original, and his indecisions have not been clarified by later copyists.

The Bohairic was made from an inferior Sahidic manuscript in the early nineteenth century. All readings of any consequence are listed by Horner.

The Arabic was made from the Sahidic, which it follows in most regards, although chapters 11-14 are not disarranged; it was therefore made from a manuscript other than the archetype of the known Sahidic codices and has a certain independent textual value. Otherwise its features are just about those to be expected in a secondary version.

The Ethiopic is divided into seventy-two "Statutes", of which the first twenty-one are the Apostolic Church Order. Statute 22 = Hippolytus's chapters 2-5, concluding with communion prayers. Chapter 6 of Hippolytus is omitted. Statutes 23-27 = chapters 8-15, with no changes in order. Statutes 28-35 = chapters 16-24, concluding with a brief additional section on the regular weekly eucharists (p. 58). Statutes 36-38 = chapters 25-26, followed by sections on the communion of the sick and on evening services (p. 58) and a repetition of chapter 26. 2, 10b-13. Statute 39 = chapter 27. Statute 40 is a long baptismal office, containing reminiscences of chapters 21-23 but opening with chapter 1, which is not in the Sahidic or Arabic. Statutes 40 (end)-48 = chapters 28-38. The remaining Statutes parallel Constitutions VIII, like the other versions, but there are certain variations; Statute 52, for instance, contains a considerable section of the Didache, a little of the Didascalia, and a bit (38. 4) of Hippolytus. At the end there is a collection of prayers.

The Ethiopic is a tertiary version, made from the Arabic. Statute 40, which gives chapter 1, was evidently derived from a different source which used the Apostolic Tradition independently, and its inclusion here was more or less accidental. But the presence of the other chapters not in the present Arabic texts is best explained by assuming that the Ethiopic was derived from an older Arabic form—which in turn presupposes an older Sahidic form; in these the omissions to avoid conflict with local usages had not yet taken place.[68]

The additional material in Statutes 5, 35 and 37-38 is printed by both Connolly and Jungklaus, although both[69] recognize the liturgical prayers in 5 to be post-Hippolytean; it is consequently not included in the present edition. But neither do the other two sections appear to be genuine. The rules in Statute 35 are so general and unobjectionable that their omission in the Sahidic and Arabic would be difficult to explain, while the reverence deacons must pay to presbyters seems to point to a later date. Similarly the description of the care of the sick and of the evening service in Statute 37 presents nothing that could have troubled the Sahidic and Arabic translators; the insertion of such widespread usages is easier to understand than their omission. And the repetition of earlier matter at the end of Statute 37 and in all of Statute 38 shows a bad textual tradition.

In general, then, the evidence of the Ethiopic is of minor consequence. In the only place where it stands alone (9. 11-12) it has a text that does not appear to be possible.

Summarizing: The original Greek of the Apostolic Tradition has not been recovered, except in small fragments. The Latin is generally trustworthy, but is incomplete. The only other primary version, the Sahidic, is likewise incomplete, and the results of the moderate abilities of its translator have been further confused in later transmission. The Arabic is a secondary text, offering little that the Sahidic does not contain. The only practically complete version,[70] the Ethiopic, is tertiary and is otherwise unreliable. All four of these versions presuppose a common Greek original, in which two different endings have been conflated. The other sources, the Constitutions, the Testament and the Canons, are frank revisions, in which the original is often edited out of recognition or even flatly contradicted. Under these conditions the restoration of a really accurate text is manifestly impossible.

None the less the material is abundant and independent enough to warrant confidence that the substance and in most cases even the original wording of Hippolytus's rules have really been preserved: only the ordination prayer for deacons presents difficulties that appear insuperable.

The chapter divisions are those of Jungklaus, altered only at chapter 22. To facilitate reference the sentences have been numbered as "verses".

THE APOSTOLIC TRADITION OF HIPPOLYTUS TRANSLATION

LAT1. [1]We have duly completed what needed to be said about "Gifts", describing those gifts which God by His own counsel has bestowed on men, in offering to Himself His image which had gone astray. [2]But now, moved by His love to all His saints, we pass on to our most important theme, "The Tradition", our teacher. [3]And we address the churches, so that they who have been well trained, may, by our instruction, hold fast that tradition which has continued up to now and, knowing it well, may be strengthened. [4]This is needful, because of that lapse or error which recently occurred through ignorance, and because of ignorant men. [5]And [the] Holy Spirit will supply perfect grace to those who believe aright, that they may know how all things should be transmitted and kept by them who rule the church.

PART I

2. [1]Let the bishop be ordained after he has been chosen by all the people. [2]When he has been named and shall please all, let him, with the presbytery and such bishops as may be present, assemble with the people on a Sunday. [3]While all give their consent, the bishops shall lay their hands upon him, and the presbytery shall stand by in silence. [4]All indeed shall keep silent, praying in their heart for the descent of the Spirit. [5]Then one of the bishops who are present shall, at the request of all, lay his hand on him who is ordained bishop, and shall pray as follows, saying:

GRE[71]3. [1]God and Father of our Lord Jesus Christ, Father of mercies and God of all comfort, who dwellest on high yet hast respect to the lowly, who knowest all things before they come to pass. [2]Thou hast appointed the borders of thy church by the word of thy grace, predestinating from the beginning the righteous race of Abraham. [3]And making them princes and priests, and leaving not thy sanctuary without a ministry, thou hast from the beginning of the world been well pleased to be glorified among those[72] whom thou hast chosen. [4]Pour forth now that power, which is thine, of thy royal Spirit, which LAT[73]thou gavest to thy beloved Servant[74] Jesus Christ, which he bestowed on his holy apostles, GREwho established the church in every place, the church which thou hast sanctified unto unceasing glory and praise of thy name. [5]Thou who knowest the hearts of all,[75] grant to this thy servant, whom thou hast chosen to be bishop, [to feed thy holy flock][76] and to serve as thy high priest without blame, ministering night and day, to propitiate thy countenance without ceasing and to offer thee the gifts of thy holy church. [6]And by the Spirit of high-priesthood to have authority to remit sins according to thy commandment, to assign the lots according to thy precept, to loose every bond according to the authority which thou gavest to thy apostles, and to please thee in meekness and purity of heart, offering to thee an odour of sweet savour. [7]Through thy Servant Jesus Christ our Lord, through whom be to thee glory, might, honour, with [the] Holy Spirit in [the] holy church, both now and always and world without end.[77] Amen.

LAT4. [1]And when he is made bishop, all shall offer him the kiss of peace, for he has been made worthy. [2]To him then the deacons shall bring the offering, and he, laying his hand upon it, with all the presbytery, shall say as the thanksgiving:

[3]The Lord be with you.

And all shall say

And with thy spirit.

Lift up your hearts.

We lift them up unto the Lord.

Let us give thanks to the Lord.

It is meet and right.

And then he shall proceed immediately:

[4]We give thee thanks, O God, through thy beloved Servant Jesus Christ, whom at the end of time thou didst send to us a Saviour and Redeemer and the Messenger of thy counsel. [5]Who is thy Word, inseparable from thee; through whom thou didst make all things and in whom thou art well pleased. [6]Whom thou didst send from heaven into the womb of the Virgin, and who, dwelling within her, was made flesh, and was manifested as thy Son, being born of [the] Holy Spirit and the Virgin. [7]Who, fulfilling thy will, and winning for himself a holy people, spread out his hands when he came to suffer, that by his death he might set free them who believed on thee. [8]Who, when he was betrayed to his willing death, that he might bring to nought death, and break the bonds of the devil, and tread hell under foot, and give light to the righteous, and set up a boundary post, and manifest his resurrection, taking bread and giving thanks to thee said: [9]Take, eat: this is my body, which is broken for you. And likewise also the cup, saying: This is my blood, which is shed for you. [10]As often as ye perform this, perform[78] my memorial.

[11]Having in memory, therefore, his death and resurrection, we offer to thee the bread and the cup, yielding thee thanks, because thou hast counted us worthy to stand before thee and to minister to thee.

[12]And we pray thee that thou wouldest send thy Holy Spirit upon the offerings of thy holy church; that thou, gathering them

into one, wouldest grant to all thy saints who partake to be filled with [the] Holy Spirit, that their faith may be confirmed in truth, that we may praise and glorify thee. [13]Through thy Servant Jesus Christ, through whom be to thee glory and honour, with [the] Holy Spirit in the holy church, both now and always and world without end.[79] Amen.

5. [1]If anyone offers oil, he shall give thanks as at the offering of the bread and wine, though not with the same words but in the same general manner,[80] saying:

[2]That sanctifying this oil, O God, wherewith thou didst anoint kings, priests and prophets, thou wouldest grant health to them who use it and partake of it, so that it may bestow comfort on all who taste it and health on all who use it.

6. [1]Likewise, if anyone offers cheese and olives, let him say thus:

[2]Sanctify this milk that has been united into one mass, and unite us to thy love. [3]Let thy loving kindness ever rest upon this fruit of the olive,[81] which is a type of thy bounty, which thou didst cause to flow from the tree unto life for them who hope on thee.

[4]But at every blessing shall be said:

Glory be to thee, with [the] Holy Spirit in the holy church, both now and always and world without end. [Amen.]

8.[82] [1]But when a presbyter is ordained, the bishop shall lay his hand upon his head, while the presbyters touch him, and he shall say according to those things that were said above, as we have prescribed above concerning the bishop, praying and saying:

[2]God and Father of our Lord Jesus Christ, look upon this thy servant, and grant to him the Spirit of grace and counsel of a presbyter,[83] that he may sustain and govern thy people with a pure heart; [3]as thou didst look upon thy chosen people and didst command Moses that he should choose presbyters, whom thou didst fill with thy Spirit, which thou gavest to thy servant. [4]And now, O Lord, grant that there may be unfailingly preserved amongst us the Spirit of thy grace, and make us worthy that, believing, we may minister to thee in simplicity of heart, praising thee. [5]Through thy Servant Jesus Christ, through whom be to thee glory and honour, with [the] Holy Spirit in the holy church, both now and always and world without end. Amen.

9. [1]But the deacon, when he is ordained, is chosen according to those things that were said above, the bishop alone in like manner laying his hands upon him, as we have prescribed. [2]When the deacon is ordained, this is the reason why the bishop alone shall lay his hands upon him: he is not ordained to the priesthood but to serve the bishop and to carry out the bishop's commands. [3]He does not take part in the council of the clergy; he is to attend to his own duties and to make known to the bishop such things as are needful. [4]He does not receive that Spirit that is possessed by the presbytery, in which the presbyters share; he receives only what is confided in him under the bishop's authority.

[5]For this cause the bishop alone shall make a deacon. [6]But on a presbyter, however, the presbyters shall lay their hands because of the common and like Spirit of the clergy. [7]Yet the presbyter has only the power to receive; but he has no power to give. [8]For this reason a presbyter does not ordain the clergy; but at the ordination of a presbyter he seals while the bishop ordains.

[9]Over a deacon, then, he shall say as follows:

[10]O God, who hast created all things and hast ordered them by thy Word, the Father of our Lord Jesus Christ, whom thou didst send to minister thy will and to manifest to us thy desire; [11]grant [the] Holy Spirit of grace and care and diligence to this thy servant, whom thou hast chosen to serve the church and to offer TESTin thy holy sanctuary[84] the gifts that are offered to thee ETHby thine appointed high priests,[85] TESTso that serving without blame[86] and with a pure heart he may be counted worthy of this exalted office,[87] by thy goodwill, praising thee continually. [12]Through thy Servant Jesus Christ, through whom be to thee glory and honour, with [the] Holy Spirit, in the holy church, both now and always and world without end. Amen.[88]

SAH10. [1]On a confessor, if he has been in bonds for the name of the Lord, hands shall not be laid for the diaconate or the presbyterate, for he has the honour of the presbyterate by his confession. But if he is to be ordained bishop, hands shall be laid upon him.

[2]But if he is a confessor who was not brought before the authorities nor was punished with bonds nor was shut up in prison, but was insulted (?) casually or privately for the name of

the Lord, even though he confessed, hands are to be laid upon him for every office of which he is worthy.[89]

[3]The bishop shall give thanks [in all ordinations][90] as we have prescribed. [4]It is not,[91] to be sure, necessary for anyone to recite the exact words that we have prescribed, by learning to say them by heart in his thanksgiving to God; but let each one pray according to his ability. [5]If, indeed, he is able to pray competently with an elevated prayer, it is well. [6]But even if he is only moderately able to pray and give praise, no one may forbid him;[92] only let him pray sound in the faith.

11.[93] [1]When a widow is appointed, she shall not be ordained but she shall be appointed by the name. [2]If her husband has been long dead, she may be appointed [without delay]. [3]But if her husband has died recently, she shall not be trusted; even if she is aged she must be tested by time, for often the passions grow old in those who yield to them.

[4]The widow shall be appointed by the word alone, and [so] she shall be associated with the other widows; hands shall not be laid upon her because she does not offer the oblation nor has she a sacred ministry.[94] [5]Ordination is for the clergy on account of their ministry,[95] but the widow is appointed for prayer, and prayer is the duty of all.

GRE[96]12. [1]The reader is appointed by the bishop's giving him the book, for he is not ordained.

SAH13. [1]Hands shall not be laid upon a virgin, for it is her purpose alone that makes her a virgin.

14. Hands shall not be laid upon a subdeacon, but his name shall be mentioned that he may serve the deacon.

15. If anyone says, "I have received the gift of healing", hands shall not be laid upon him: the deed shall make manifest if he speaks the truth.

PART II

16. [1]New[97] converts to the faith, who are to be admitted as hearers of the word, shall first be brought to the teachers before the people assemble. [2]And they shall be examined as to their reason for embracing the faith, and they who bring them shall testify that they are competent to hear the word. [3]Inquiry shall then be made as to the nature of their life; whether a man has a wife[98] or is a slave.[99] [4]If he is the slave of a believer and he has his master's permission, then let him be received; but if his master does not give him a good character, let him be rejected. [5]If his master is a heathen, let the slave be taught to please his master,[100] that the word be not blasphemed.[101] [6]If a man has a wife or a woman a husband, let the man be instructed to content himself with his wife and the woman to content herself with her husband. [7]But if a man is unmarried, let him be instructed to abstain from impurity, either by lawfully marrying a wife or else by remaining as he is.[102] [8]But if any man is possessed with demons, he shall not be admitted as a bearer until he is cleansed.

[9]Inquiry shall likewise be made about the professions and trades of those who are brought to be admitted to the faith. [10]If a man is a pander,[103] he must desist or be rejected. [11]If a man is a sculptor or painter, he must be charged not to make idols; if he does not desist he must be rejected. [12]If a man is an actor or pantomimist, he must desist or be rejected. [13]A teacher of young children had best desist, but if he has no other occupation, he may be permitted to continue. [14]A charioteer, likewise, who races or frequents races, must desist or be rejected. [15]A gladiator or a trainer of gladiators, or a huntsman [in the wild-beast shows],[104] or anyone connected with these shows, or a public official in charge of gladiatorial exhibitions must desist or be rejected. [16]A heathen priest or anyone who tends idols must desist or be rejected. [17]A soldier of the civil authority[105] must be taught not to kill men and to refuse to do so if he is commanded, and to refuse to take an oath;[106] if he is unwilling to comply, he must be rejected. [18]A military commander or civic magistrate that wears the purple must resign or be rejected. [19]If a catechumen or a believer seeks to become a soldier, they must be rejected, for they have despised God. [20]A harlot or licentious man[107] or one who has castrated himself, or any other who does things not to

be named, must be rejected, for they are defiled. [21]A magician must not [even] be brought for examination. [22]An enchanter, an astrologer, a diviner, a soothsayer, a user of magic verses, a juggler, a mountebank, an amulet-maker[108] must desist or be rejected. [23]A concubine, who is a slave and has reared her children and has been faithful to her master alone, may become a hearer; but if she has failed in these matters she must be rejected. [24]If a man has a concubine, he must desist and marry legally; if he is unwilling, he must be rejected.

[25]If, now, we have omitted anything (any trade?), the facts [as they occur] will instruct your mind; for we all have the Spirit of God.

17. [1]Let catechumens spend three years as hearers of the word. [2]But if a man is zealous and perseveres well in the work, it is not the time but his character that is decisive.

18. [1]When the teacher finishes his instruction, the catechumens shall pray by themselves, apart from the believers. [2]And [all] women, whether believers or catechumens, shall stand for their prayers by themselves in a separate part of the church.

[3]And when [the catechumens] finish their prayers, they must not give the kiss of peace, for their kiss is not yet pure. [4]Only believers shall salute one another, but men with men and women with women; a man shall not salute a woman.

[5]And let all the women have their heads covered with an opaque cloth, not with a veil of thin linen, for this is not a true covering.

19. [1]At the close of their prayer, when their instructor lays his hand upon the catechumens, he shall pray and dismiss them; whoever gives the instruction is to do this, whether a cleric or a layman.

[2]If a catechumen should be arrested for the name of the Lord, let him not hesitate about bearing his testimony; for if it should happen that they treat him shamefully and kill him, he will be justified, for he has been baptized in his own blood.

20. [1]They who are to be set apart for baptism shall be chosen after their lives have been examined: whether they have lived soberly, whether they have honoured the widows, whether they have visited the sick, whether they have been active in well-doing. [2]When their sponsors have testified that they have done these

things, then let them hear the Gospel. 3Then from the time that they are separated from the other catechumens, hands shall be laid upon them daily in exorcism and, as the day of their baptism draws near, the bishop himself shall exorcise[109] each one of them that he may be personally assured of their purity. 4Then, if there is any of them who is not good or pure, he shall be put aside as not having heard the word in faith; for it is never possible for the alien to be concealed.[110]

5Then those who are set apart for baptism shall be instructed to bathe and free themselves from impurity and wash themselves on Thursday. 6If a woman is menstruous, she shall be set aside and baptized on some other day.

7They who are to be baptized shall fast on Friday, and on Saturday the bishop shall assemble them and command them to kneel in prayer. 8And, laying his hand upon them, he shall exorcise all evil spirits to flee away and never to return; when he has done this he shall breathe in their faces, seal their foreheads, ears and noses, and then raise them up. 9They shall spend all that night in vigil, listening to reading and instruction.

10They who are to be baptized shall bring with them no other vessels than the one each will bring for the eucharist; for it is fitting that he who is counted worthy of baptism should bring his offering at that time.

21. 1At cockcrow prayer shall be made over the water. 2The stream shall flow through the baptismal tank or pour into it from above when there is no scarcity of water; but if there is a scarcity, whether constant or[111] sudden, then use whatever water you can find.

3They shall remove their clothing. 4And first baptize the little ones; if they can speak for themselves, they shall do so; if not, their parents or other relatives shall speak for them. 5Then baptize the men, and last of all the women; they must first loosen their hair and put aside any gold or silver ornaments that they were wearing: let no one take any alien thing down to the water with them.

6At the hour set for the baptism the bishop shall give thanks over oil and put it into a vessel: this is called the "oil of thanksgiving". 7And he shall take other oil and exorcise it: this is called "the oil of exorcism". [The anointing is performed by a presbyter.][112] 8A deacon shall bring the oil of exorcism, and shall stand at the presbyter's left hand; and another deacon shall take the oil of thanksgiving, and shall stand at the presbyter's right hand. 9Then the presbyter, taking hold of each of those about to be baptized, shall command him to renounce, saying:

I renounce thee, Satan, and all thy servants and all thy works.

10And when he has renounced all these, the presbyter shall anoint him with the oil of exorcism, saying:

Let all spirits depart far from thee.

TEST11Then, after these things, let him give him over to the presbyter[113] who baptizes, and let the candidates stand in the water, naked, a deacon going with them likewise.[114] 12And when he who is being baptized goes down into the water, he who baptizes him, putting his hand on him, shall say thus:

Dost thou believe in God, the Father Almighty?[115]

13And he who is being baptized shall say:

I believe.

14Then

LATholding his hand placed on his head, he shall baptize him once. 15And then he shall say:

Dost thou believe in Christ Jesus, the Son of God, who was born of the Holy Ghost of the Virgin Mary, and was crucified under Pontius Pilate, and was dead and buried, and rose again the third day, alive from the dead, and ascended into heaven, and sat at the right hand of the Father, and will come to judge the quick and the dead? 16And when he says:

I believe,

he is baptized again. 17And again he shall say:

Dost thou believe in [the] Holy Ghost, and the holy church, and the resurrection of the flesh?

18He who is being baptized shall say accordingly:

I believe,

and so he is baptized a third time.[116]

[19]And afterward, when he has come up [out of the water], he is anointed by the presbyter with the oil of thanksgiving, the presbyter saying:

I anoint thee with holy oil in the name of Jesus Christ.

[20]And so each one, after drying himself, is immediately clothed, and then is brought into the church.

22.[117] [1]Then the bishop, laying his hand upon them, shall pray, saying:

O Lord God, who hast made them worthy to obtain remission of sins through the laver of regeneration of [the] Holy Spirit, send into them thy grace, that they may serve thee according to thy will; for thine is the glory, to the Father and the Son, with [the] Holy Spirit in the holy church, both now and world without end. Amen.[118]

[2]Then, pouring the oil of thanksgiving from his hand and putting it on his forehead, he shall say:

I anoint thee with holy oil in the Lord, the Father Almighty and Christ Jesus and [the] Holy Ghost.

[3]And signing them on the forehead he shall say:

The Lord be with thee;

and he who is signed shall say:

And with thy spirit.

[4]And so he shall do to each one.

[5]And immediately thereafter they shall join in prayer with all the people, but they shall not pray with the faithful until all these things are completed. [6]And at the close of their prayer they shall give the kiss of peace.

23. [1]And then the offering is immediately brought by the deacons to the bishop, and by thanksgiving he shall make the bread into an image[119] of the body of Christ, and the cup of wine mixed with water according to the likeness[120] of the blood, which is shed for all who believe in him. [2]And milk and honey mixed together for the fulfilment of the promise to the fathers, which spoke of a land flowing with milk and honey; namely, Christ's flesh which he gave, by which they who believe are nourished like babes, he making sweet the bitter things of the

heart by the gentleness of his word. [3]And the water into an offering in a token of the laver, in order that the inner part of man, which is a living soul, may receive the same as the body.

[4]The bishop shall explain the reason of all these things to those who partake. [5]And when he breaks the bread and distributes the fragments he shall say:

The heavenly bread in Christ Jesus.

[6]And the recipient shall say, Amen.

[7]And the presbyters—or if there are not enough presbyters, the deacons—shall hold the cups, and shall stand by with reverence and modesty; first he who holds the water, then the milk, thirdly the wine. [8]And the recipients shall taste of each three times, he who gives the cup saying:

In God the Father Almighty;

and the recipient shall say, Amen. [9]Then:

In the Lord Jesus Christ;

[and he shall say, Amen. [10]Then:

In][121] [the] Holy Ghost and the holy church;

and he shall say, Amen. [11]So it shall be done to each.

[12]And when these things are completed, let each one hasten to do good works,
SAHand to please God and to live aright, devoting himself to the church, practising the things he has learned, advancing in the service of God.

[13]Now we have briefly delivered to you these things concerning the holy baptism and the holy oblation, for you have already been instructed concerning the resurrection of the flesh and all other things as taught in Scripture.[14]Yet if there is any other thing that ought to be told [to converts], let the bishop impart it to them privately after their baptism; let not unbelievers know it, until they are baptized: this is the white stone of which John said: "There is upon it a new name written, which no one knoweth but he that receiveth the stone".

PART III

GRE[122]25.[123] [1]Widows and virgins shall fast frequently and shall pray for the church; presbyters, if they wish, and laymen may fast likewise. [2]But the bishop may fast only when all the people fast.

26. [1]For it constantly happens that some one wishes to make an offering—and such a one must not be denied—and then the bishop, after breaking the bread, must in every case taste
SAHand eat it with the other believers. [2][At such an offering] each shall take from the bishop's hand a piece of [this] bread before breaking his own bread. [This service has a special ceremonial][124] for it is "a Blessing", not "a Thanksgiving", as is [the service of] the Body of the Lord.[125] [3]But before drinking, each one,
LATas many of you as are present,
SAHmust take a cup and give thanks over it,
LATand so go to your meal.

[4]But to the catechumens is given exorcised bread, and each of them must offer the cup. [5]No catechumen shall sit at the Lord's Supper.

[6]But at each act of offering, the offerer must remember his host, for he was invited to the latter's home for that very purpose. [7]But when you eat and drink, do so in an orderly manner and not so that anyone may mock, or your host be saddened by your unruliness, but behave so that he may pray to be made worthy that the saints may enter his dwelling: "for ye", it is said, "are the salt of the earth".

[8]If the offering should be one made to all the guests jointly,[126] take your portion from your host [and depart]. [9]But if all are to eat then and there, do not eat to excess, so that your host may likewise send some of what the saints leave to whomsoever he will and [so] may rejoice in the faith.

[10]But while the guests are eating, let them eat silently, not arguing, [attending to][127] such things as the bishop may teach, but if he should ask any question, let an answer be given him; and when he says anything, everyone in modest praise shall keep silence until he asks again.

[11]And even if the bishop should be absent when the faithful meet at a supper, if a presbyter or a deacon is present they shall eat in a similar orderly fashion, and each shall be careful[128] to take the blessed bread from the presbyter's or deacon's hand; and in the same way the catechumens shall take the same exorcised bread.

[12]But if [only] laymen meet, let them not act presumptuously, for a layman cannot bless the blessed bread.[129]

[13]Let each one eat in the name of the Lord; for this is pleasing to the Lord that we should be jealous [of our good name] even among the heathen, all sober alike.[130]

27. [1]If anyone wishes to give a meal to widows of mature years, let him dismiss them before evening. [2]But if, on account of existing conditions,[131] he cannot [feed them in his house], let him send them away, and they may eat of his food at their homes in any way they please.

28. [1]As soon as first-fruits appear, all shall hasten to offer them to the bishop. [2]And he shall offer them, shall give thanks and shall name him who offered them, saying:

[3]We give thee thanks, O God, and we offer thee the first-fruits; which thou hast given us to enjoy, nourishing them through thy word, commanding the earth to bring forth her fruits for the gladness and the food of men and all beasts. [4]For all these things we praise thee, O God, and for all things wherewith thou hast blessed us, who for us adornest every creature with divers fruits. [5]Through thy Servant Jesus Christ, our Lord, through whom be to thee glory, world without end. Amen.

[6]Only certain fruits may be blessed, namely grapes, the fig, the pomegranate, the olive, the pear, the apple, the mulberry, the peach, the cherry, the almond, the plum. [7]Not the pumpkin, nor the melon, nor the cucumber, nor the onion nor garlic nor anything else having an odour.

[8]But sometimes flowers too are offered; here the rose and the lily may be offered, but no other.

[9]But for everything that is eaten shall they [who eat it] give thanks to the Holy God, eating unto His glory.

29. [1]Let no one at the paschal season[132] eat before the offering is made,[133] otherwise he shall not be credited with the fast. [2]But if any woman is with child, or if anyone is sick and cannot fast for two days, let such a one, on account of his need, [at least] fast on Saturday, contenting himself with bread and water. [3]But if anyone on a voyage or for any other necessary cause should not know the day, when he has learned the truth he shall postpone his fast until after Pentecost. [4]For the ancient type has passed away, and so the [postponed] fast [of Numbers 9. 11] in the second month has ceased, and each one ought to fast in accord with his knowledge of the truth.[134]

30. [1]Each of the deacons, with the subdeacons, shall be alert on the bishop's behalf, for the bishop must be informed if any are sick so that, if he pleases, he may visit them; for a sick man is greatly comforted when the high priest is mindful of him.

SAH33.[135] [1]Let the deacons and the presbyters assemble daily at the place which the bishop may appoint; let the deacons [in particular] never fail to assemble unless prevented by sickness. [2]When all have met they shall instruct those who are in the church, and then, after prayer, each shall go to his appointed duties.

34. [1]No exorbitant charge shall be made for burial in the cemetery, for it belongs to all the poor; only the hire of the grave-digger and the cost of the tile [for closing the niche in the catacombs] shall be asked. [2]The wages of the caretakers are to be paid by the bishop, lest any of those who go to that place be burdened [with a charge].

PART IV

35. [1]Let all the faithful, whether men or women, when early in the morning they rise from their sleep and before they undertake any tasks, wash their hands and pray to God; and so they may go to their duties. [2]But if any instruction in God's word is held [that day], everyone ought to attend it willingly,[136] recollecting that he will hear God speaking through the instructor and[137] that prayer in the church enables him to avoid the day's evil; any godly man ought to count it a great loss if he does not attend the place of instruction, especially if he can read.

[3]If a [specially gifted][138] teacher should come, let none of you delay[139] to attend the place where the instruction is given, for grace will be given to the speaker to utter things profitable to all, and thou wilt hear new things,[140] and thou wilt be profited by what the Holy Spirit will give thee through the instructor; so thy faith will be strengthened by what thou hearest, and in that place thou wilt learn thy duties at home; therefore let everyone be zealous to go to the church, the place where the Holy Spirit abounds.[141]

36. [1]But if on any day there is no instruction, let everyone at home take the Bible and read sufficiently in passages that he finds profitable.

[2]If at the third hour thou art at home, pray then and give thanks to God; but if thou chance to be abroad at that hour, make thy prayer to God in thy heart. [3]For at that hour Christ was nailed to the tree; therefore in the old [covenant] the law commanded the showbread to be offered continually for a type of the body and blood of Christ, and commanded the sacrifice of the dumb lamb, which was a type of the perfect Lamb; for Christ is the Shepherd, and he is also the Bread that came down from heaven.

[4]At the sixth hour likewise pray also, for, after Christ was nailed to the wood of the cross, the day was divided and there was a great darkness; wherefore let [the faithful] pray at that hour with an effectual prayer, likening themselves to the voice of him who prayed [and] caused all creation to become dark for the unbelieving Jews.

[5]And at the ninth hour let a great prayer and a great thanksgiving be made, such as made[142] the souls of the

righteous ones, blessing the Lord, LATthe God who does not lie, who was mindful of his saints and sent forth his Word to enlighten them. [6]At that hour, therefore, Christ poured forth from his pierced side water and blood, and brought the rest of the time of that day with light to evening; so, when he fell asleep, by making the beginning of another day he completed the pattern of his resurrection.

[7]Pray again before thy body rests on thy bed.

[8]At midnight arise, wash thy hands with water and pray. [9]And if thy wife is with thee, pray ye both together; but if she is not yet a believer, go into another room and pray, and again return to thy bed; be not slothful in prayer.

[10]He who has used the marriage bed is not defiled; for they who are bathed have no need to wash again, for they are clean. [11]By signing thyself with thy moist breath, and so spreading spittle[143] on thy body with thy hand, thou art sanctified to thy feet; for the gift of the Spirit and the sprinkling with water, when it is brought with a believing heart as it were from a fountain, sanctifies him who believes.

[12]It is needful to pray at this hour; for those very elders who gave us the tradition taught us that at this hour all creation rests for a certain moment, that all creatures may praise the Lord: stars and trees and waters stand still with one accord, and all the angelic host does service to God by praising Him, together with the souls of the righteous. [13]For this cause believers should be zealous to pray at this hour; for the Lord, testifying to this, says: "Behold at midnight is a cry, Behold the Bridegroom cometh! Rise up to meet him!"; and he adds insistently: "Watch ye therefore, for ye know not at what hour he cometh".

[14]And at cockcrow rise up and pray likewise, for at that hour of cockcrow the children of Israel denied Christ, whom we have known by faith; by which faith, in the hope of eternal life at the resurrection of the dead, we look for his Day.

[15]And so, all ye faithful, if ye thus act, and are mindful of these things, and teach them to one another, and cause the catechumens to be zealous, ye can neither be tempted nor can ye perish, since ye have Christ always in your minds.

37.[144] [1]But imitate him always, by signing thy forehead sincerely; for this is the sign of his Passion, manifest and approved against the devil if so thou makest it from faith; not that thou mayest appear to men, but knowingly offering it as a shield. [2]For the adversary, seeing its power coming from the heart, that a man displays the publicly formed image of baptism,[145] is put to flight; not because thou spittest, but because the Spirit in thee breathes him away. [3]When Moses formed it by putting the blood of the Paschal lamb that was slain on the lintel and anointing the side-posts, he signified the faith which now we have in the perfect Lamb.

38.[146] [1]And so, if these things are accepted with thanksgiving and right faith, they give edification in the church and eternal life to believers. [2]I counsel that these things be kept by all who know aright; for over all who hear the apostolic tra[dition]
SAHand keep it, no heretics or any other man will prevail to lead them astray. [3]For the many heresies have increased because their leaders would not learn the purpose of the apostles but acted according to their own wills, following their lusts and not what was right.

[4]Now, beloved, if we have omitted anything, God will reveal it to those who are worthy, guiding the holy church to its mooring in [God's] quiet haven.

LATER ADDITIONS

ETH24. [1]On Saturday and Sunday the bishop shall whenever possible give the people the bread with his own hand, while the deacons break it. [2]The presbyters too shall break the bread to be delivered; and whenever a deacon approaches a presbyter he shall hold out his robe,[147] and the presbyter shall take the bread and deliver it to the people with his hand.

[3]On other days they shall give the bread as the bishop determines.

On this section compare p. 31. It may be further observed that section 2 is pretty clearly an addition.

ETH26. [14]In time of need the deacon shall be diligent in giving the blessed bread[148] to the sick. [15]If there is no presbyter to give out what is to be distributed, the deacon shall pronounce the thanksgiving and shall supervise[149] those who carry it away, to make sure that they attend to their duty and [properly] distribute the blessed food; the distributors must give it to the widows and the sick. [16]Whoever is entrusted with the duty by the church[150] must distribute it on the same day; if he does not, he must [at least] do so on the next day with the addition of what is then given him. [17]For [it is not his own property]; it is given him only [in trust] as bread for the poor.

[18]When evening has come and the bishop is present, the deacon shall bring in a lamp. [19]Then the bishop, standing in the midst of the believers, before giving thanks shall first give the salutation:

> The Lord be with you all.

[20]And the people shall say:

> [And] with thy spirit.

[21]And the bishop shall say:

> Let us give thanks to the Lord.

[22]And the people shall say:

It is meet and right:

Majesty, exaltation and glory are due to Him.

23But they shall not say "Lift up your hearts", for that belongs to the oblation. 24And he prays thus, saying:

We give thee thanks, O God, because thou hast enlightened us by revealing the incorruptible light. 25So we, having finished the length of a day, and being come to the beginning of the night, satisfied with the light of the day that thou hast created for our satisfaction; and now, since by thy grace we lack not a light for the evening, we sanctify thee and we glorify thee. 26Through thine only Son our Lord Jesus Christ, through whom be to thee with him glory and might and honour with [the] Holy Spirit, now, etc.[151]

27And they shall all say: Amen.

28Then, rising up after supper, the children and virgins having prayed, they shall sing psalms. 29Then the deacon, holding the mixed cup of the offering, shall say a Hallelujah Psalm.[152] 30Then, the presbyter having commanded, "And also such-and-such Psalms", after the bishop has offered the cup[153] with the proper thanksgiving, all shall say "Hallelujah" as the Psalms are sung. 31And they shall say:

We praise Him who is God most high;

Glorified and praised is He,

Who founded the world with a single word.[154]

32Then, when the Psalm is completed, he shall give thanks over the bread, and shall give the fragments to all the believers.

On these sections compare p. 31. An evening service, that included bringing in the lamp, is widespread in early Christianity and is eventually derived from Judaism; the particular service described here is a prelude to a congregational agape. There is nothing in sections 18-32 that necessarily implies a date later than Hippolytus, but the ceremony is badly placed between the private agapes and the equally private meals for the widows, and it is followed by a duplication of 26. 2, 10-12.

LAT31. 1The faithful, early in the morning, as soon as they have awaked and arisen, before they undertake their tasks shall pray to God and so may then go to their duties. ²But if any instruction in the word is held, let each give first place to that, that he may attend and hear the word of God, to his soul's comfort; so let each one hasten to the church, where the Spirit abounds.

32. ¹But let each of the faithful be zealous, before he eats anything else, to receive the eucharist; for if anyone receives it with faith, after such a reception he cannot be harmed even if a deadly poison should be given him. ²But let each one take care that no unbeliever taste the eucharist, nor a mouse nor any other animal, and that nothing of it fall or be lost; for the body of Christ is to be eaten by believers and must not be despised. ³The cup, when thou hast given thanks in the name of the Lord, thou hast accepted as the image of the blood of Christ. ⁴Therefore let none of it be spilled, so that no alien spirit may lick it up, as if thou didst despise it; thou shalt be guilty of the blood, as if thou didst scorn the price with which thou hast been bought.[155]

In the Oriental versions the position of chapters 31-32 between chapters 30 and 33 is impossible. Chapter 30 addresses the church's officers, chapters 31-32 individuals, chapters 33-34 the officers, and chapter 35 individuals again; chapter 31, in addition, is only a condensation of 35. 1-3. But the Hauler manuscript clears up the difficulty. In it chapter 32 is followed immediately by the Latin A form of 37. 1-38. 2a, breaking off at the end of a leaf with "apo" (for "apostolic"). The next leaf begins with "God" in the middle of 36. 5, and the text continues through 36, gives the Latin B form of 37. 1-38. 2a and breaks off this time with "tra" for "tradition". So two versions of the work were current with different endings; in one chapter 30 was followed by 31-32 and the A conclusion, in the other it was followed by 33-35 and the B conclusion. In the Hauler manuscript both endings were reproduced, although the leaves containing the last two sentences of the first and a considerable part of the second have been lost. In the Oriental versions—or the Greek codex underlying them—the glaring duplication caused by the ending after 32 was suppressed, although the doubling of 35. 1-3 in 31 remained.

Since chapter 34 is unmistakably Roman and consequently Hippolytean, the longer ending is original; chapter 33, moreover, is perfectly in place after chapter 30. So Schwartz[156] and Jungklaus are correct in holding[157] that chapter 32 is not by Hippolytus; the only alternative would be to assume that he issued two versions of his book with different endings—a difficult supposition that would leave unexplained why the very important practice stressed in chapter 32 is omitted in the longer version.

On the other hand it is true, as Connolly argues,[158] that the rules of chapter 32 are truly third-century. The custom according to which each Christian kept the consecrated eucharist in his house and received it each morning is attested in Tertullian's *To his Wife* II, 5, and the reason given (Mark 16. 18) for receiving fasting is not that of the later church (compare on chapter 29); Connolly observes further that the home reservation of consecrated wine as well as consecrated bread is unknown elsewhere.

Very curious, too, is the phrase "when *thou* hast given thanks" in section 3, for the section as a whole is addressed to the laity. Is there here some reminiscence of earlier corporately celebrated eucharists, like the agapes in chapter 26? Or are 3-4 a later addition, addressed to the clergy? Or is there textual confusion?

NOTES1

Characteristic of Hippolytus's style are his frequent summaries of the progress of his treatises; compare 16. 25; 23. 13; Philosophumena, Proem.; i, 23. 4, etc.

The opening sentence is obscure, but Connolly's explanation (pp. 161-162) appears the most likely: Man, made in God's image, went astray, but through the Incarnation God restored humanity by presenting to Himself Christ, the perfect Man.

2. On the phrase translated "most important theme" compare Connolly, p. 161; the original Greek word was presumably κορυφή.

3. If the "churches" are the different Roman congregations—an unusual sense—Hippolytus speaks simply as a bishop; if the meaning is "at Rome and elsewhere" he speaks not only as a bishop but as a teacher of eminent authority.

4. The "lapse or error" is the Zephyrinus-Callistus "schism". As Hippolytus speaks of it as a recent event, the date of the treatise cannot be far from 217.

PART I
Ordination

2

THE BISHOP

An episcopal election is still in the hands of the "multitude" (compare Acts 6. 2), the clergy as yet having no distinct voice in theory. Rather curiously no qualifications are given for the bishop; contrast, e.g., 1 Timothy 3. 2-7 or the expansions in the Constitutions and the Testament. The bishop's functions are essentially the same as in the Ignatian Epistles: as the embodiment of his church's unity he is the centre and head of all its activities, whether in teaching, worship, or discipline.

The title "high priest", however, is not used by Ignatius, and in the extant Christian literature first occurs in Tertullian, *On Baptism* 17 (*ca.* 205); Hippolytus also uses "high-priesthood" of the episcopal office in Philosophumena, Proem. 6. Similarly Tertullian calls the presbyters "priests" in his *Exhortation to Chastity* 7, 11 (*ca.* 210), and in 9. 2 of our treatise Hippolytus describes their work as "priesthood".

This appearance of sacerdotal titles for Christian ministers—something that is foreign to the New Testament—was a consequence of the adoption of sacrificial terms for Christian worship:[159] sacrifices are offered by priests. So Didache 13. 3 describes the prophets as "your high priests" (compare 15. 1), while Ignatius (*Philadelphians* 4) writes "one altar, as one bishop". Consequently it is more than probable that "high priest" and "priest" were in common—although by no means universal—use among Christians by the middle of the second century. Hippolytus's distrust of innovations corroborates this; apart from anti-modalist additions the terminology of his consecration prayer can scarcely be thought to depart much from the forms in use in his younger days.

Otherwise the bishop is said to "feed the flock", a New Testament phrase[160] that was of course traditional; to Hippolytus it would include both correct teaching of doctrine and faithful administration of the sacraments. Since in Philosophumena IX, 7 he inveighs fiercely against Callistus's claim to absolve grave sins, "to remit" here can refer only to minor offences. "To assign the lots" strictly construed would mean "to appoint the clergy", but compare on 9. 1. "To loose every bond" is probably only a traditional liturgical generality.

THE CHRISTIAN "SACRIFICES"

Sacrificial terms in the New Testament, except when used to describe the Atonement, are employed within Christianity only in a transferred sense: the Christian sacrifices are either acts of righteousness,[161] the rendering of prayer and praise,[162] or gifts given to fellow-Christians.[163] In the post-apostolic age this last sense was popular and in one particular application it was made a definitely technical term. Christian worship and Christian social life centred in a "table-bond"; the specifically Christian act of worship was the eucharist, which in apostolic times was regularly celebrated in conjunction with a meal of some sort,[164] and even in Hippolytus's day had not lost all traces of the earlier custom (chapters 5-6). But the Christians were extremely fond of other common meals as well, the "agapes", of a less sacred but still definitely religious nature (chapter 26). In all of these meals the amount of food required was considerable, and providing it naturally entailed real expense. To supply this food, consequently, was a meritorious act, which not only satisfied the needs of the brethren but enabled the church to hold a liturgical service, at which the food was placed in the midst of the congregation and "blessed".[165] Hence the various foods were naturally called "offerings", and from this it was only a short step to calling the service itself a "sacrifice".

The word first appears in Didache 14. 1-2, where it is used of the eucharist or (more probably) the eucharist-agape. When the term was definitely adopted into the Christian vocabulary, its further definition in Old Testament language was inevitable. Here the nearest analogue might have been found in the "peace-offerings", which were eaten by those who offered them. But the Christians did not usually follow Levitical distinctions closely, and Hippolytus (3. 5) speaks of the bishop as "propitiating God's countenance", language that more properly belongs to the "sin-offerings".

A special type of Christian offering were the first-fruits (chapter 28), which were likewise solemnly presented and "blessed" by the bishop. There were again explicit Old Testament analogies, but in Christianity "sacrifice" did not permanently become a term for this custom.

2. Notice of the election and of the Sunday appointed for the consecration was sent to the neighbouring churches, whose bishops would naturally attend as far as they were able.

3. The assent of the people was given by acclamation; according to the Canons in the form "We choose him!" The explicit injunction that the presbyters must not join in the imposition of hands should be noted; the Arabic omits the prohibition, perhaps accidentally, but the Canons read "One of the bishops and presbyters shall be chosen to lay his hand upon his head". Compare on 9. 5-8.

In the Constitutions the deacons hold the book of the Gospels over the person to be consecrated.

The Jewish background of this prayer is extremely marked, and 2-3 may well have been taken bodily from some synagogue formula; Christianity is regarded as the orderly continuation of Old Testament Judaism.

4. "Royal" (more precisely "princely") renders ἡγεμονικός, taken from the Septuagint version of Psalm 51. 12 (50. 14).

The Epitome's abbreviation in this passage avoids suggesting that until a definite moment the Son did not possess the Spirit (Connolly, p. 151). The unabbreviated text is practically only a combination of Matthew 3. 16 and John 20. 22, but the result is so definitely anti-modalistic that it is probably the work of Hippolytus; the language is over-precise for a prayer.

5. "Thou who knowest the hearts of all" is from Acts 1. 24, but such exact Scriptural language is more characteristic of the fourth century than the third. While the emphasis is on the bishop's offering the "gifts", his prayers for his flock are certainly not excluded as part of his high-priestly ministry (Hebrews 7. 25, etc.).

6. The "odour of sweet savour" is the offering of a holy life, as in Romans 12. 1.

7. The doxology is that given in the Epitome and presupposed in the Canons and Testament, with the substitution of "through whom" (so the other sources) for "with whom" (a peculiarity of the Epitomist). After "honour" the Latin and Ethiopic insert "to the Father and the Son". "Servant" as a liturgical title for Christ comes from Acts 4. 27, 30; the later versions naturally substitute "Son".

The Sahidic and the Arabic omit the consecration prayer entirely, presumably because it did not accord with local use. The Canons paraphrase Hippolytus's form slightly; the Constitutions and the Testament enlarge it greatly. For the sake of comparison Sarapion's prayer may be given:

> Thou who didst send the Lord Jesus for the gain of the whole world, thou who didst through him choose the apostles, thou who generation by generation didst ordain holy bishops, O God of truth, make this bishop also a living bishop, worthy (?) of the succession of the holy apostles, and give to him grace

> and divine Spirit, that thou didst freely give to all thine own servants and prophets and patriarchs: make him to be worthy to shepherd thy flock, and let him still continue unblamably and unoffendingly in the bishopric.

It will be observed that here the references to the Old Testament are almost non-existent and that there is no mention of high-priestly functions.

4-6
THE EUCHARIST

Fundamental for any comprehension of the first liturgical history of the eucharist is the fact that among Jews a "blessing" of food is without exception a "thanksgiving"; a Jew never says "Bless this food", but always "Blessed be God". So in the New Testament, when such a blessing is in question, εὐχαριστέω and εὐλογέω are used without distinction; compare, e.g., Mark 8. 6-7.

The various Jewish blessings in their oldest literary forms are collected in the Mishnah tractate *Berakhoth*;[166] this was finally compiled in the third century, but most of its contents are much earlier; note in chapter 8 the account of the pre-Christian controversy between the schools of Hillel and Shammai. The form of all the blessings is the same; after the opening words of praise the worshipper recites the particular act of God for which thanksgiving is due. So over bread the formula is:

> Blessed be thou, O God, King of the universe, who hast brought forth bread from the ground;

and over wine:

> Blessed be thou, O God, King of the universe, who hast created the fruit of the vine.

There is no real reason to doubt that these were the words used by Christ at the Last Supper when he "gave thanks"; Mark 14. 25 takes up the blessing used over the cup.

To eat without thanksgiving was a sin, and he who did so at least violated God's law commanding thankfulness. But most Jews would also have held that unblessed food is unfit for consumption, and that pronouncing the benediction removes this quasi-uncleanness, i.e., "hallows" it: "Nothing is to be rejected, if it be received with thanksgiving; for it is sanctified through the word of God[167] and prayer".[168] In other words, the act of thanksgiving was construed as having a consecratory effect, potent even for ordinary food and therefore especially potent for sacred food. So St Paul writes in 1 Corinthians 10. 16: "The cup of thanksgiving over which we give thanks, is it not a communion of the blood of Christ?" In Hippolytus the same conception appears unambiguously in 21. 6 and 23, but it also underlies his use of "thanksgiving" in 4. 2 and 10. 4.

Accordingly, since at the Christians' greatest liturgical service the essential formula was a solemn thanksgiving, the service itself and food consecrated at the service both came to be called simply "The Thanksgiving" or (in Greek) "The Eucharist".[169] And—certainly in the second century, since Hippolytus gives the formula—the eucharistic prayer was prefaced by the invitatory, "Let us make our thanksgiving to the Lord", and this in turn by the appropriate words, "Lift up your hearts".

Since extempore prayer was still largely practised (4), the contents of the Christian thanksgivings naturally varied widely, but it would appear inevitable that at first, in accord with Christ's example, God's provision of food for men was the normal topic: the beautiful prayer in the Didache is formed on this model, which Hippolytus follows closely in chapters 5-6. But the thought of food in the bread and wine was overshadowed by the thought of redemption, and even in the Didache the earthly species only typify the salvation wrought in Christ. In chapter 4 of Hippolytus the "table" form of the blessing is abandoned altogether for the praise of Christ's redeeming works, and the same is true of practically all later liturgies. As is entirely natural, Hippolytus's thanksgiving concludes with reciting the work of Christ most vividly in mind at the moment: his institution of the rite that the church was engaged in celebrating.[170]

The evidence of the later liturgies shows us that the purely Christian objects of thanksgiving in Hippolytus were by no means the only ones for which God was blessed; thanks could be given with entire appropriateness to the Father for any of His benefits from creation on. For such prayers Jewish synagogue formulas provided models that were freely utilized; compare, e.g., Constitutions VII, 33-38. These thanksgivings often included (VII, 35, 3) or culminated in the hymn of Isaiah 6. 3 ("Sanctus"), and in this way this hymn passed into the Christian eucharistic prayers, to become an all but universal feature in them. In the liturgy in the Constitutions it stands at a place that shows its origin, at the close of the (Jewish) thanksgivings for Old Testament benefits (VIII, 12, 27) and before the (Christian) thanksgivings for Christ's incarnate acts.

After the completion of the thanksgiving (4. 10) Hippolytus makes certain additions. 4. 11 declares that in performing the rite the church remembers Christ according to his command: this is the germ of what in the later liturgies is known as the "anamnesis". And the offering is formally presented to God; this likewise reoccurs regularly and is called the "oblation". Either or both of these features could have been used in any eucharistic prayer from the earliest time.

4. 12, however, shows a later concept. In the age of Hippolytus the consecratory effect of thanksgiving was growing unfamiliar, and a special petition was thought needful in order that the bread and wine might truly be made "a communion" of the body and blood of Christ. The liturgy's thought is simple: if earthly food is truly to become "spiritual" food,[171] God must send upon it the Spirit. The prayer is phrased accordingly, and is the first known instance of what is technically known as the "invocation", universal in Eastern liturgies, although absent from the present Roman. But the testimony of Irenaeus shows that in the late second century at Rome the invocation was regarded as the truly consecratory formula,[172] and Hippolytus continues Irenaeus' tradition.

Hippolytus's use of the invocation shows that only bread and wine are offered to God at the oblation. For his doctrine of communion see on 23. 1.

2. "All the presbytery" join with the bishop in offering the gifts; the "concelebration" of a later terminology. The custom is derived from a time when the local monarchical episcopate was not yet established and the presbyters were normal officiants at worship.[173] They act in their corporate capacity; compare on chapter 8.

4. If 11 is construed strictly, the "we" of this prayer should be "we, the bishop and presbyters". But the plural pronoun originally—and probably in Hippolytus's opinion also—meant "all we Christians in this congregation"; compare 4. 12, "your sacrifice" in Didache 14 and the explicit language in Justin, Dialogue 116-117. "Messenger of thy counsel" is from the Septuagint of Isaiah 9. 6; it recurs in Hippolytus's Daniel commentary (III, 9, 6) and is used here as an anti-modalist term.

5. This whole sentence is anti-modalist.

6. As in 3. 4 the language is more theological than liturgic.

7. Christ's hands were spread out in appeal (Isaiah 65. 2, Lamentations 1. 17).

8. The "boundary post" is the Cross, dividing the realms of life and death.

9. The terms in Christ's words regarding the bread and the cup are given liturgical balance by introducing κλώμενον, "which is broken", after "body"; this addition found its way into many manuscripts of 1 Corinthians 11. 24.

10. The terseness of this phrase is effective. In the Latin translator's "commemorationem facitis" the indicative is certainly a mistake,[174] while his "perform a memorial" may be merely a Latinistic simplification of "do this in memory of me"; the Pseudo-Ambrosian *De Sacramentis* has similarly "commemorationem facietis" and the present Roman liturgy "memoriam facietis". By what follows the phrase here means "recall to our mind".

11. To "death" in 1 Corinthians 11. 26 "resurrection" has been added; later liturgies at this point expand freely. Later liturgical development also connected "memory" and "offer" closely, pleading Christ's death before the Father.

12. The prayer for unity echoes the habitual Jewish prayers for the return of all Israel to Palestine; compare the Didache.

13. Compare on 3. 7.

In this prayer as a whole the accumulation of phrases in 5-6 is largely due to Hippolytus, who may likewise be responsible for parts of 7-8. But, even as it stands, it is noteworthy for its sobriety and directness, both characteristic of the later Roman liturgy until Gallican floridity affected it.

The liturgical influence of this prayer has been incalculable. It is the basis of the liturgy in the Constitutions, through which it determined the form and in part the wording of the great Eastern liturgies, St James,[175] St Basil and St Chrysostom. In the other Eastern rites its influence is usually perceptible, though less fundamental, while in the Ethiopic church it is still used almost unchanged. In the West, however, later eucharistic conceptions led to a different type of liturgy.

Hippolytus gives only the vital part of the ceremony, which otherwise was presumably much as it is described in Justin, *Apology* 67. But perhaps at a consecration service the opening lessons and instruction were omitted.

5-6

This blessing at the eucharist of food other than the bread and wine is a remnant of the primitive custom when the rite included a meal; in Hippolytus's day, presumably, the cheese and olives were eaten at the service and part of the oil was sipped, the remainder being reserved for anointing the sick.[176] Perhaps only Hippolytus's exaggerated reverence for the past preserved the usage, which at any rate soon disappeared. None of the other versions of his treatise retain chapter 6, for which the Canons[177] substitute a blessing of first-fruits. In the Testament the oil is blessed solely for the sick,[178] and this is probably the conception in the Ethiopic and the Canons. The Sahidic and Arabic replace all of 4-6 with a note that the bishop should follow "the (local) custom".

The usual Old Testament background to these prayers need hardly be pointed out.

The prayer at the blessing of the oil has real affinities with the prayer still used in the Roman church for blessing the "oil of the sick" at the bishop's Maundy Thursday eucharist.

6

2. This ingeniously worded prayer has no parallel.

3. Compare Zechariah 4. 12.

4. Compare the Jewish use of fixed *initial* clauses in benedictions.

8

PRESBYTERS

"Presbyter" is a technical term in Judaism, which early Christianity took over.[179] The Jewish conceptions at the beginning of the Christian era are best seen in the Mishnah tractate *Sanhedrin*:[180] the presbyters, in virtue of their divinely instituted office (Exodus 24. 9), preserved, interpreted and applied the received tradition of God's revelation, and so were the divinely appointed rulers of Israel. In consequence, every Jewish community, even the smallest, had its presbytery,[181] which exercised all local governmental functions. When a vacancy occurred, the presbytery elected a new member; if he had served as a presbyter elsewhere, he was simply caused to "take his seat"; if not, the presbytery ordained him by the imposition of hands. Individual presbyters had no authority, which was possessed solely by the body as a whole; this principle was maintained so rigorously that there were not even regular presiding officers.[182] If a priest was elected as a presbyter, he was ordained like anyone else.[183] The same seems to have been true of the Rabbis[184] before A.D. 70; after that year they took over what was left of the presbyters' duties and were always ordained.

It must be borne in mind that the Jewish presbyters were community officers, not cult officials. They could determine how worship should be conducted, but as presbyters they had no special share in conducting it: this was the equal privilege of all male Israelites.[185] In particular, while the presbyters, among their other duties, administered the affairs of the local synagogue, to define them as "elders of the synagogue" is totally to misunderstand them.

The introduction of the presbyterial system into Christianity offers a complicated problem, into which it is unnecessary to enter here. It is enough to note that in the New Testament when the office is fully developed—as in Acts and the Pastoral Epistles—the Jewish analogies are evident. In Hippolytus's ordination prayer the Jewish origin is explicitly recognized; so much so that the institution of the office is attributed to Moses, whose seventy elders possessed the same gifts and functions as their Christian namesakes. Accordingly the essential duties of a presbyter are simply to "sustain and govern",[186] and no other specific gifts are prayed for. So it is really conceivable that

Hippolytus's formula reproduces the substance of a Jewish ordination prayer.

In Christianity, however, the most important service was a feast in which the whole community joined, while in Judaism the (numerous) sacral meals were held by each family separately.[187] Hence the Christian presbyters could be called on for duties unlike those of the Jewish officials; as the leaders of the community they might well appear as the leaders of the community's feast. And in fact, as the "charismatic" prophets, teachers, etc., gradually disappeared, the presbyters became the normal officiants at the eucharist.[188] So it was only a question of time until they acquired sacerdotal titles; compare 9. 2 in our treatise.

The introduction of the local monarchical episcopate transformed the presbytery from the ruling body into a mere council of advice for the bishop, and so reduced radically the importance of its members. They had a voice in disciplinary affairs, and they clung tenaciously to their share in offering the eucharist and in the ordination of a new member to their ranks. Otherwise during the late second and third centuries their duties[189] might be little more than honorary, and in most communities[190] the presbyters probably devoted their weekdays to secular occupations; in contrast to the bishop and the deacons.

1. In 1 Timothy 4. 14, as in Judaism, ordination is by the presbytery. A different conception appears in 2 Timothy 1. 6, and harmonization of the two produced ordination by the bishop *and* the presbytery, the practice still maintained in the Roman and Anglican Communions. For Hippolytus's theory compare 9. 4-8.

2. The verbs "sustain and govern" are the cognates of the nouns translated "helps, governments" in 1 Corinthians 12. 28. But in 1 Corinthians *two* offices are meant.

3. Compare Exodus 24. 9-11. That these elders were "filled with the Spirit" is from Numbers 11. 25, but the specific mention of this in an ordination prayer seems Christian rather than Jewish.

4. The bishop here includes himself with the presbytery, perhaps a survival of a form used in pre-episcopal days.

In the Ethiopic this prayer is reproduced almost unchanged. The Epitome has:

Almighty lord, who through Christ hast created all things and through him hast foreseen all things; look even now upon thy holy church, and give it increase, and multiply its rulers, and grant them might to labour with word and work for the building up of thy people. And now look upon this thy servant, who by the voice and judgment of all the clergy is chosen for the presbytery, and fill him with the Spirit of grace and counsel, that he may sustain and govern thy people with a pure heart—as thou didst look upon thy chosen people and didst command Moses that he should choose presbyters, whom thou didst fill with the Spirit—that he, being filled with powers of healing and words of teaching in meekness, may diligently instruct this thy people with a pure mind and a willing soul, and may blamelessly complete the ministrations for thy people. Through thy Christ, with whom be to thee glory and worship, with the Holy Spirit, world without end. Amen.

This prayer is evidently Hippolytus's, somewhat enlarged and slightly revised, and the only real difference is that the bishop no longer associates himself with the presbytery. The Constitutions merely expand the Epitome's prayer still further with a recital of God's attributes. In the Testament there is an independent expansion of Hippolytus's form, but again without significant variations. Sarapion has still another paraphrase, but one equally centred about the presbyter's teaching office.

The Sahidic and the Arabic, however, provide that the prayer used for the consecration of a bishop shall also be used at the ordination of a presbyter. With this the Canons agree, reading: "When a presbyter is ordained, let all things take place for him as take place for the bishop, with the exception of the word 'bishop'. The bishop is in every regard like the presbyter, apart from the throne and the ordination, for to the latter no power to ordain is given". This evidence is in accord with the well-known fact that the introduction of the monarchical episcopate came later in Egypt than elsewhere.

9
DEACONS

The development of the diaconate in the first century is extremely obscure, but in the Pastoral Epistles and 1 Clement "presbyters" are divided into "bishops and deacons"—in these works the three terms are never used together—indicating specializations within the presbyterate. Some presbyters were especially concerned in "overseeing" the community and others with "serving" it—particularly in charitable works; compare the "governments" and "helps" in 1 Corinthians 12. 28. When monarchical episcopacy was introduced, the now more or less supernumerary "overseers" were less important than the "servers", who became the personal assistants of the bishops. The respective status in the third century is set forth in Didascalia, chapter 9 (= Constitutions II, 26, 4-7): "Let the bishop ... be honoured by you as God.... The deacon is with you as a type of Christ, so let him be loved by you. Let the deaconess be honoured by you as a type of the Holy Spirit. Let the presbyters be looked on by you as a type of the apostles".

1. The reference is apparently to chapter 2, with no explanation how choice by the people is reconciled with 3. 6. The Sahidic, the Testament and the Canons agree with the Latin, but the Arabic, Ethiopic and the Constitutions speak only of the bishop. But the close relations between the bishop and the deacons would seem to make his freedom of choice necessary.

Does the absence of any provision for election in chapter 8 indicate that the presbyters were still chosen by the presbytery?

2-4. Any (surviving?) remnant of the conception of deacons as "serving presbyters" is dismissed summarily.

5-8. Hippolytus is attempting to reconcile a ceremonial survival of the days when presbyters ordained with the doctrine that ordination is the prerogative of bishops. The result is incoherent; if a presbyter has no power to "give", what is said of the "common and like Spirit" is pointless. And, although the passage appears intact (or expanded) in the other versions, 7-8 read like a later addition. But perhaps these are a theory of Hippolytus's, glossed on a traditional phrase.

10-12. The original text of this passage is very uncertain. The Latin breaks off with "offere", and the following words in the

Ethiopic and the Testament stress what in Hippolytus is a minor and not characteristic function of the deacons (4. 2), while their chief duties are ignored. Moreover, neither the Constitutions, the Canons nor Sarapion have anything corresponding; all three—in widely different terms—petition for "faithfulness" and "wisdom"; all three, incidentally, quote Acts 6. It is worth noting that none of the sources call the deacons "Levites"; this title[191] appears to come in a later age when—through the change from local to diocesan episcopacy—the deacons became the assistants of the presbyters.

The Ethiopic[192] and the Constitutions speak of the diaconate as a preparation for the presbyterate: this conception belongs to the fourth, not the third, century.

10
CONFESSORS

1. A true confessor is, *ipso facto*, a presbyter. This declaration—which other conceptions have altered in the Ethiopic and the Constitutions—follows logically from the original definition of a presbyter's duties: since his primary function is to bear witness to the truth, and since no witness can be more impressively borne than when in danger of death, a confessor proves that he has the Spirit of the presbyterate. Hence ordination would be otiose.

A still earlier theory is that set forth in Hermas, *Visions* III, i, where the correct ranks of those who occupy the "bench" (of the clergy) is given as "confessors,[193] prophets, presbyters", as three distinct orders; in Hippolytus the prophets disappear and the confessors are merged with the "regular" presbyters.

In the third century, as confessors multiplied, observance of this rule would have overloaded the presbyterate to an impracticable degree,[194] although in the small community of Hippolytus the difficulty would not be felt and the traditional practice could be maintained inviolate. But elsewhere the modification in Constitutions VIII, 23 was no doubt widely accepted: the office of a confessor was one of great dignity,[195] but it did not include its holder among the clergy.[196] The Ethiopic compromises: a confessor is not yet a presbyter, but can claim episcopal ordination to the presbyterate as a right.

2. Hippolytus treats these "minor" confessors as the Constitutions treat the true confessors. The other sources (except the Constitutions) deal with them more generously. In the Ethiopic they can *claim* ordination to the diaconate, in the Arabic and the Canons to the presbyterate, in the Sahidic to any office of which they are worthy; compare the Testament.

The Canons have a curious provision for a confessor who is a slave (and therefore incapable of receiving ordination); such a one is "a presbyter for the congregation", even though he does not receive "the insignia of the presbyterate".

CONCLUSION OF ORDINAL

3. "At every ordination the eucharist must be offered."

4. Compare Justin, *Apology* 67, where the "president" offers prayers "according to his ability" (ὅση δύναμις αὐτῷ), and Tertullian, *Apology* 30: "we pray ... without a monitor, for our prayers are from the heart". But extempore prayer in no way excludes frequent use of traditional formulas.

11-15
MINOR ORDERS

In the major orders an endowment of the Spirit is sought by the imposition of hands; in the minor orders persons are officially admitted to the exercise of gifts that they already possess.

11

2-3. The eventual source is 1 Timothy 5. 1-16.

4-5. In 1 Timothy the widows engage both in prayer (verse 5) and in active work (verse 10). In the Didascalia and Constitutions these duties are divided: prayer is the sole task of the "widows", while those to whom the active work is committed are called "deaconesses". The latter, except that they have no part in the liturgy, correspond in all respects to the deacons, and so naturally receive an ordination, while the "widows" are merely "named". So, before the distinction was established, ordination of (all?) widows was presumably fairly usual; otherwise the vigour of Hippolytus's protest is difficult to explain.

In Rome, unlike Syria, active church work by women was discountenanced and the deaconesses did not make their appearance. On the general subject of women's work the Didascalia is a mine of information.

12

Men who could read easily and clearly from a manuscript were not too common, so that the reader had a position of some dignity. The Constitutions, in fact, make a major order of the office and the prayer (VIII, 22) beseeches "the prophetic Spirit", suggesting that readers were expected to give some exposition and teaching. Both the Constitutions and the Testament treat readership as a step toward higher advancement. In the Sahidic the reader is given St Paul's Epistles; Schwartz (p. 32) thinks this is original.

13

For the development of the status of virgins in the church reference must be made to the special literature. Hippolytus, in marked contrast to the Testament, dismisses the subject very briefly and refers to virgins again only in 25. 1, although this brevity of treatment in a law book does not prove lack of practical interest in the subject. As the "purpose" was publicly announced, it corresponded to the later formal vow.

14

The account in Acts 6 was generally interpreted as limiting the number of deacons in any place to seven, far too few for effective service in large churches. So each deacon was given an assistant to "serve" him; compare chapter 30. But even this was inadequate in very large communities, and at Rome *ca.* 250 the seven deacons and their subdeacons were further assisted by forty-two acolytes ("followers").[197] The subdiaconate eventually became a major order and it is so treated in the Constitutions and the Testament.

15

The gift of healing (1 Corinthians 12. 28, etc.) was the only one of the primitive charismatic gifts to survive into the third century in its original form, and in Hippolytus its purely charismatic nature is still recognized; not only is there no ordination but the healer is not even "named". But healers in the specialized form of "exorcists" form a minor order in Rome a generation later.[198] One of their most important functions was to assist in preparing catechumens for baptism; compare 20. 3.

PART II
Baptism

16-20
CATECHUMENS

In the apostolic age converts were accepted with little question and were baptized immediately on profession of faith;[199] the missionary zeal of the new religion, heightened by the expectation of the end of the world, sought only to compel men to come in. Naturally this enthusiasm was always tempered with common sense—no teacher could have baptized every applicant—but the doors were opened wide, and the New Testament gives no hint of any formal training before reception. The hope that defects would be made up by Christian grace was doubtless fulfilled to a surprising degree, but it was also often grievously disappointed: men were admitted into Christianity who neither understood its teachings nor desired to follow them, and it was from this class that Gnosticism and other vagaries drew their recruits. The account in Acts 8. 18-24 is typical.

The result was a violent reaction that made entry into the church extremely difficult, and no one was permitted baptism until he had passed through a long and searching probation called the "catechumenate". As it appears fully developed in the early third century, it must reach far back into the second or perhaps even into the first.

16

1. "Hearers" is perhaps used here in its later technical sense as a title for catechumens in their first stage. In Hippolytus the "word" that they are permitted to hear does not include the Gospel (20. 2); elsewhere they were allowed to remain at the Sunday service until all the liturgical lessons had been read and the sermon had been preached. The "teachers" were those employed in the instruction of the catechumens; they were not necessarily clerics (19. 1) and did not form a special class.

2-24. The reason for most of these rules is self-evident.

13. Greek education included much time spent on Homer, whose mythology the Christians naturally regarded as unedifying. But the permission given to schoolmasters to continue their calling in case of necessity shows that no one took the Homeric deities very seriously.

17. In many cases soldiers were utilized only for police duty, but Christian soldiers were always in danger of being given tasks inconsistent with their religion. Hippolytus probably does not consider the rather infrequent possibility of soldiers being sent to defend the frontiers against barbarians. The "oath" invoked heathen deities.

18. Judges and military officers were constantly called on to pronounce and inflict capital punishment. They were also inextricably involved in the support of emperor-worship.

19. A man who was already a soldier could be accepted under the conditions of 17. But no believer was permitted voluntarily to expose himself to such temptations.

23. Since the woman in such a case had no power to alter her condition, Hippolytus's rule is sensible and humane.

24. Men, who could control their conduct, were granted no such concession.

25. A remnant of the older charismatic teaching; Compare 38. 4. It is conjoined somewhat oddly with these detailed legalistic prescriptions; the right to judge spiritually may be exercised only where the law is not explicit. And only the clergy exercise the gift.

17

A three years catechumenate has parallels in later practice, but it represents about the maximum.

18

1. Separation of catechumens from believers and men from women was carried out rigorously throughout the Patristic age.

3-4. Contrast 22. 6. The kiss of peace marked the close of the service that preceded the eucharist (e.g., Constitutions VIII, 11, 9).

5. 1 Corinthians 11. 10.

19

1. The imposition of hands was partly in blessing, partly in exorcism (20. 3). In later days the first of these impositions was regarded as the formal admission to the catechumenate.

2. A universal Patristic teaching.

20

2. Hippolytus knows only two classes of catechumens, the hearers and those "set apart". Subsequently the latter were called "elect", "competent" or "enlightened", and an intermediate class ("kneelers") was introduced. Hippolytus says nothing about the duration of this last stage, but four to six or more weeks is later common.

3. Exorcism before baptism was universally practised and has survived in some form or other in practically all the traditional baptismal liturgies. It lacks New Testament precedent, but is based on the dualism found in John 14. 30, etc., according to which this world—and so all its unregenerate inhabitants—is under the sway of Satan and his angels. In Hippolytus's community the exorcisms were presumably performed by the teachers, as he does not recognize exorcists as a separate class (compare on chapter 15).

4. The text of the last clause is so uncertain that the meaning of the whole is dubious. The Testament, however, asserts that the episcopal exorcism is bound to make an unworthy candidate betray himself, and there is no reason to doubt that Hippolytus believed the same.

5. The final selection and instruction took place on the Thursday before Easter. "Bathing" was done in a public bath-house, with a supplementary "washing" at home; compare John 13. 10.

6. Most religions, as well as Judaism, regarded a menstruous woman as unclean.

7. All believers fasted on Good Friday (29. 1); for the catechumens the fast was probably thought to be purifying.

8. The Testament gives a lengthy form for this last pre-baptismal exorcism. Popular belief in the life-giving power of breath (Genesis 2. 7, etc.) was very widespread; compare 36. 11. Mark 7. 34 may have been specially in mind.[200] The "seal" was the sign of the cross. Compare chapter 37.

9. No further opportunity was given to contract defilement.

10. This direction, misunderstood in the Arabic and Ethiopic, is explained by 23. 1-2. Those about to be baptized brought with them as their first Christian "offering" the bread, wine, milk and

honey needed for the baptismal eucharist. The Testament reduces this offering to one loaf from each of them. The rule should not be explained from chapter 32, which is not by Hippolytus.

21
THE BAPTISMAL CEREMONY

1. Hippolytus gives no form for the blessing of the water, but the Constitutions (VII, 43) direct an elaborate thanksgiving, concluding with the words "Sanctify this water and give it grace and power", etc. Clement of Alexandria (*Pedagogue* I, vi (50, 4)) appears to presuppose a petition for the descent of the Logos into the font.

2. The superior sanctity of "living" water is a common belief, and the Testament and the Canons allow no other for baptism. Compare Didache 7. 1.

3. Every non-Jew in the Graeco-Roman world was so accustomed to the public baths that the baptismal usage would not suggest the slightest impropriety.

5. To Hippolytus the ornaments as "alien" carry contagion. The Jews have a similar prohibition for women bathing after ceremonial impurity, but the reason given is that complete contact with the water is prevented.

6. The first mention of anointing in connection with baptism is in Tertullian, *On Baptism* 7 (*ca.* 205). He explains the practice as derived from the Old Testament anointing of priests, and in view of 1 Peter 2. 9 and Revelation 1. 6; 5. 10[201] this may well express the original meaning of the ceremony. Or it may have been thought to convey the gift of the Spirit, as in 1 Samuel 16. 13, or may rest on more general conceptions of anointing as consecration, or may even be somehow connected with the title "Christ" (= "The Anointed One"). But, whatever the origin, unction after baptism is found practically everywhere in Christendom after the third century.

In Hippolytus the blessing is still a thanksgiving and the oil is named accordingly. In the Constitutions (VII, 44) the formula is petitionary,[202] and the oil is called "mystical". The common later title for this oil—to which other substances, such as balsam, are often added—is "chrism". The Latin formula for blessing it still includes a solemn thanksgiving.

7. The anointing before baptism is derived from the ancient belief in the curative powers of oil, from which its use in religious healing (Mark 6. 13, James 5. 14) was developed. To Hippolytus

this oil aids in the final and supreme exorcism, and it is exorcised, not blessed, and derives its name from its purpose. In later Latin usage it is called "oil of the catechumens".

The Constitutions note (VII, 22, 3) that if the oils are lacking "the water is sufficient". And this was the universal belief.

9. Some form of renunciation of Satan is a feature in all traditional baptismal liturgies.

10. Cyril of Jerusalem (*Catechetical Lectures* 20, 3) says that this anointing is performed "from the very hairs of your head to your feet". By 22. 2 Hippolytus has probably the same conception.

11. The pronouns are ambiguous and confusing, but the sense seems to be that the presbyter who performs the actual baptism stands on the bank of the stream (or the edge of the font), while the deacon stands in the water with the candidate, to instruct and assist him.

12-18. In the Jewish rites that require complete immersion (the baptism of a proselyte, the cleansing of a woman, etc.) the ceremony is performed entirely by the person concerned in the presence of a proper witness; i.e., such a rite is simply an extension of the Old Testament prescriptions[203] that certain impurities must be removed by bathing. Early Christianity shared this conception, and in New Testament Greek the middle voice is used for the act of baptism in Acts 22. 16, 1 Corinthians 6. 11; 10. 2; compare the reading of D and Old Latin manuscripts in Luke 3. 7, "to be baptized in his presence". In Hippolytus the presbyter acts to the extent of laying his hand on the candidate's head, but he uses no baptismal formula.[204] In the Jewish rites the person after immersion utters a benediction; in Hippolytus each immersion is preceded by a declaration of belief. In the apostolic church this declaration certainly had the form "Jesus is Lord" (Romans 10. 9, etc.) and there was only one immersion. The additional confessions of the Father and the Spirit appear in Didache 7. 1,[205] and each was presumably accompanied by the corresponding immersion that Hippolytus directs.

Each of these three confessions was then further expanded, so producing the various baptismal creeds. The one in use at Rome in the early fourth century—the basis of the later "Apostles' Creed"—can be reconstructed accurately from Rufinus' *Exposition*, and agrees closely with the form in the Latin version of Hippolytus, the only significant addition being "and the forgiveness of sins" near the close. This clause, in fact, seems to be due eventually to Hippolytus's arch-enemy, Callistus, to express a doctrine that the former abhorred. On the other hand, there is some evidence that the official Roman creed *ca.* 200 did not contain "and the holy church", on which Hippolytus lays stress (6. 4; 23. 10); this clause may be his own addition to protest—against Callistus—that the "holy" church should not contain sinners. Later Roman Christianity adopted both phrases with no feeling of incongruity; compare Cyprian's "forgiveness of sins through the holy church".[206]

19. This anointing, like the former, presumably covered the whole body.

20. In the later Patristic church at this point the newly baptized put on white garments, which they wore for seven days.

22

CONFIRMATION

Hippolytus contributes little to clarifying the difficult subject of confirmation. In Acts 8. 17 and 19. 6 the rite conveys the gift of the Spirit, but Hippolytus's prayer, which cites Titus 3. 5, follows the Pauline-Johannine[207] doctrine in attributing this gift to baptism, in accord with the special immersion after confessing the Spirit. So only grace for service is besought. But, as in Acts, the essential ceremony is the imposition of hands, so that the anointing and the sign of the cross are only supplementary rites. Curiously enough, however, only the anointing was preserved in both the Latin and the Orthodox Eastern churches.

For the use of the Lord's Prayer after baptism see on 23. 14.

23

THE BAPTISMAL EUCHARIST

Compare the distinction between the baptismal and the regular eucharist in Justin, *Apology* 65 and 67 and in Didache 9-10 and 14.

1. The conception of consecration by thanksgiving is stated so baldly that the Latin ("gratias agat panem quidem in exemplum") is wholly unidiomatic, but in all probability the prayer normally included an invocation like that in 4. 12. Here, in place of the "spiritual food" language in 4. 12, the result of the consecration is expressed in the terms of the institution. Yet Hippolytus appears to shrink a little from calling the species absolutely the body and blood of Christ: the bread is the "image" (ἀντίτυπον) of the body and the cup the "likeness" (ὁμοίεμα) of the blood. The former word is used in the same way by Cyril of Jerusalem (23, 20; as an adjective) and the latter by Sarapion in his first oblation before the words of institution; compare "figura" in Tertullian, *Against Marcion* III, 19 and IV, 40, and the prayer in the Constitutions (VIII, 12, 39) that the species may be made to "appear" (ἀποφάναι) as the body and blood. None of this language, however, is "symbolic" in the modern sense; whatever unlikeness theologians[208] might feel existed between the symbols and the things signified was overshadowed by the realistic connection that existed between them. But in the earlier Patristic period the deeper nature of this connection was left unexplored.

2. Tertullian (*chaplet* 3, *Against Marcion* I, 14) and Clement of Alexandria (*Pedagogue* I, vi (45, 1)) bear contemporary testimony to the custom of giving new Christians milk and honey, so the rite must have been widespread. It is not in the Constitutions or the Testament, but the other sources have it. And the 24th canon of the Third Council of Carthage (397) reads: "The first-fruits, namely milk and honey, which are offered on a most solemn day for the mystery of infants,[209] although offered on the altar should have a blessing of their own, that they may be distinguished from the sacrament of the Lord's body and blood".

Clement of Alexandria, like Hippolytus, cites the Old Testament prophecies of the promised land,[210] so the meaning of the rite was to assure the participants of a share in salvation.

But Hippolytus adds a further explanation of his own; the milk represents Christ's flesh and the honey his gentleness. The Canons—possibly with a misrecollection of Isaiah 7. 15—interpret the food as proper for the newly born.

3. The purpose of the water is to extend the baptismal washing into the inner man; a somewhat pedantic ceremony that reappears only in the Ethiopic, although the Testament applies the theory to the water in the mixed eucharistic chalice.

5. This is the earliest known formula for eucharistic administration.

7-11. What is most curious about these directions is that the sacramental wine is not distinguished in administration from the other two cups; the other versions correct this.[211] Perhaps in this ceremony there has survived something of the tradition in the earliest text of Luke 22. 19-20, where the whole emphasis is laid on the bread.

The little four-clause creed is interesting.

12. An admirable little summary of Christian duty.

13. Hippolytus (compare I. 1) refers to some earlier work or works of his own, possibly *Concerning God and the Resurrection*, whose title is listed on his statue.

14. By the "white stone" (Revelation 2. 17) evidently something very concrete is implied. This cannot be any part of the creed, which is recited while baptism is in progress, and so the Testament's explanation of the secret as the doctrine of the resurrection[212] is excluded. The only other possibility would appear to be the Lord's Prayer, on which Hippolytus is strangely silent. Christians of this age regarded the Prayer as having an almost magical efficacy. It was, moreover, allowed to none but the baptized and was first uttered by Christians immediately after their baptism,[213] a custom which in the light of Romans 8. 15 and Galatians 4. 6 may actually go back to apostolic times.

PART III
Church Laws

25. Fasting is here conceived to intensify prayer's efficacy. The widows and virgins were especially dedicated to the work of intercession.

The other versions have "pray *in* the church", but the Greek gives a more primitive impression.

The bishop, on account of the nature of his duties, was not permitted to vow a fast to last for any set time; he might, of course, abstain from food informally if he wished. Good Friday and Holy Saturday (chapter 29) were the only fixed fast-days, but special fasts for all might be directed on any special occasion.

26

THE AGAPE

The agape, or "love-feast", was a Christian meal of a definitely religious character. Since both Tertullian (*Apology* 39) and Clement of Alexandria (*Pedagogue* II, i (4-7)) speak of it as an established Christian custom, its origin must lie far behind the third century, and the importance and liturgical colouring given by the Evangelists to the accounts of the feedings of the multitudes[214] are explicable only as reflecting deep first-century interest in the rite. Its origin in Christianity, consequently, must be primitive, while the Gospels indicate that in the apostolic church it was regarded as a continuation of the (many) meals shared by Christ and his disciples. The emphasis on the numbers who were satisfied by the bread and fish, taken together with Acts 6. 1-3[215] and the later history of the agape, show that a primary purpose of these meals was to provide food for the needy: it is presumably from this aim that the name "love-feast" was derived. And the Gospel accounts indicate that in the agapes Christ was felt to be acting as head of his household: that he was in some manner present.

The agape and the eucharist, consequently, were closely associated; in 1 John 6 the feeding of the multitudes leads into the elaborate eucharistic discourse. So Ignatius uses "eucharist" and "agape" as synonyms,[216] while "The Lord's Supper", the term employed by St Paul[217] and later writers generally for the eucharist, is Hippolytus's title here for the agape. The confusion was due to the fact that in the first century the eucharist was generally celebrated in conjunction with an agape; indeed, in 1 Corinthians 11 it is clear that the Corinthians were stressing the banquet elements of their common meals so strongly that their eucharistic aspect had been forgotten.[218] Hence in Jude 12 the "love-feasts" are most naturally understood to be the combined agape-eucharists.

During the second century the rites were separated, the eucharist being transferred to the morning, while the agape normally remained as an evening meal, although it could of course be held at any hour. But Hippolytus preserves remnants of the old association; as regards the eucharist the oil, cheese and olives of chapters 5-6, as regards the agape the title "Lord's Supper" and details of the ceremonial.

According to Hippolytus's description the agapes are meals given by individuals in their own homes; the host provides the food and invites the guests, who in return are expected to pray for him. Each person breaks his own bread and "offers" his own cup; this is in accord with the rule in Berakhoth vi. 6 for the less solemn meals among the Jews: "If men sit for a meal, each shall pronounce the blessing for himself; but if they recline, one shall pronounce the blessing for them all". This procedure, moreover, appears to throw light on the account in 1 Corinthians 11, where the church is blamed because "each taketh before other his own supper" (verse 21) and the remedy prescribed is "wait for one another" (verse 33); it is difficult to see how the Corinthian disorders could have arisen if there were a single officiant. In Hippolytus orderliness is procured by the presence of a cleric—preferably the bishop, although a deacon will suffice—who presides over the supper and begins it by blessing and distributing a loaf specially named; this ceremony is superadded to a ritual otherwise complete in itself, and appears to be a local Roman custom.

1-2. In the earliest Christianity "blessing" and "thanksgiving" were indistinguishable,[219] but to Hippolytus they are no longer always synonyms; perhaps the "blessing" was accomplished by signing with the cross, as in the Canons.

After blessing, the bishop breaks the loaf, eats a portion himself, and distributes the remainder to all the baptized members of the company: a procedure exactly like that of the eucharist. In the earlier combined service, in fact, this bread would have been actually eucharistic, for which after the separation "blessed" bread was substituted to enable the traditional agape ceremonial to continue with a minimum of external change. The final separation must have been comparatively recent, for Hippolytus feels obliged to emphasize the difference between the two rites; in later times there was no danger of confusion, and his translators consequently do not seem to have grasped his point.

2. The breaking of each one's bread would be accompanied by a proper benediction.

3. Roughly parallel is Berakhoth vi. 6: "If wine is brought during a meal, each one must pronounce the blessing for himself".

4. For the distinction between "blessing" and "exorcism" of objects, compare 21. 6-7. The Arabic and Ethiopic substitute

"blessed bread", even for the catechumens. Whether the catechumens also broke their "own" bread is left uncertain. "Offer" is here a mere synonym for "give thanks", a usage not found in the other versions.

5. Perhaps the catechumens stood during the agape; perhaps they ate at a separate table.

6. Each blessing at an agape must include a prayer for the host, who is thus repaid for his bounty. For "offer" the other versions substitute "eat", spoiling the force.

7. From 1 Corinthians 11. 21 to the final abolition of the agapes in Christianity (in the eighth century?) there were constant complaints of disorderly conduct at these meals; Clement of Alexandria (*l.c.*) for this reason objects to their name. Hippolytus cites Matthew 5. 13.

8. ἀποφόρητον is simply "that which is carried away" and is used in its etymological sense; other meanings, such as the associated "a gift given to dinner guests", are immaterial here. The "apoforetum" began like the regular agape with the distribution of the blessed bread and (presumably) with public benedictions over bread and wine, but the rest of the meal was eaten at each one's home.

9. The Gospel accounts of the miraculous feedings lay similar stress on gathering up the fragments.

10. The complete dominance of the meal by the bishop would seem to make the above warnings against disorder needless; as Hippolytus pictures it an agape would have been the reverse of hilarious.

11-12. Compare Ignatius, *Smyrnaeans* 8. 1: "Let that be counted a genuine[220] eucharist that is held by the bishop or by someone to whom he gives permission"; for the last clause as regards the agapes Hippolytus simply substitutes "or one of the clergy". In later theory only a priest can "bless", and any formula that can be pronounced validly by a deacon can be pronounced just as "validly", although perhaps not "licitly", by a layman. But this distinction between "valid" and "licit" would not have been drawn by Ignatius or Hippolytus; what a Christian cannot do licitly he cannot do at all. Evidently Hippolytus regards the blessed bread as of the essence of the agape.

The Testament agrees in general with Hippolytus. In the Canons the agape becomes a memorial feast (ἀνάλημψις) for the dead. It is forbidden on Sunday. The participants first make their communions and then meet for the meal. The bread distributed is "exorcised";[221] explained as signed with the cross. The presence of a cleric—normally a presbyter—while desirable does not seem to be quite essential.

27

The widows were special objects of the church's charity, but precautions had to be taken lest even they became disorderly. The "existing conditions" may refer to persecutions, but the phrase is more simply understood of the donor's inability to entertain a large party in his own home; compare the *apoforetum*.

28

Hippolytus, like Didache 13. 3, regards the law of Deuteronomy 18. 4 as binding on Christians; he says nothing, however, of an obligation to tithe. The Jewish background of his prayer is evident; compare particularly Berakhoth vi. 2 "through whose word all things come to pass", and Rabbi Jehudah's formula in vi. 1 "who hast created divers fruits". The only Christian touch is at the end, and the rest of the prayer may have been taken bodily from a Jewish source.

The reasons for the distinctions in 6-7 are probably irrecoverable, but vegetables of the gourd family were favoured food among ascetics of the gnostic type. Perhaps Canticles 2. 1 gave the lily and the rose their privileged status.

In Hippolytus's day these first-fruits constituted the chief source of support for the clergy. A writer—probably Hippolytus himself—in Eusebius V, 28. 10-12 speaks with detestation of the payment of money salaries by heretics to their leaders.

29

On Good Friday and Holy Saturday all Christians were expected to fast according to their ability; a meritorious act whose credit would be lost if terminated too soon.[222] If neglected through ignorance it could be made up later, but not between Easter and Pentecost, when all fasting was everywhere forbidden to orthodox Christians. It may be observed that Hippolytus's conception of the repeal of the "ancient law" extends only to the particular date set by Numbers 9. 11; otherwise it is still fully binding. Compare Didache 8. 1.

This fast, it should be noted, is directed only before the Easter communion; later writers, like the Testament, treat the breach of a fast (from midnight, generally) before any communion as a mortal sin. Compare, further, chapter 32.

30

Hippolytus presupposes a congregation still small enough to enable the bishop to visit the sick personally, but large enough to make his visit a great event to the sick person.

33

This daily session of the presbyters was the Christian "sanhedrin", to which individuals brought their problems and controversies for "instruction". At these gatherings, in addition, the clergy received assignments for their duties of that day; in these latter the deacons were more important than the presbyters and their absence a more serious fault.

34

Callistus is commemorated by the Roman catacombs that still bear his name; probably dissatisfaction with his rival's regulations led Hippolytus to treat this rather specialized subject. The other versions miss the point of the "tiles"—on which compare Connolly, pp. 116-119—and adapt the rules to local burial customs; the Testament, for instance, discusses embalming.

PART IV
Lay Devotions

The devotional life of a layman is centred around the declaration of Psalm 119. 164, "Seven times a day do I praise thee", at rising, at the third, sixth and ninth hours, at bedtime, at midnight and at cockcrow. This distribution corresponds approximately to the later "canonical hours", but in Hippolytus's day these prayers were still wholly private.

35

1. Following the general—especially Jewish—belief demanding ceremonial purification before approaching God, Hippolytus requires hand-washing (at least) at morning and midnight; the Canons extend this rule to all prayer. Tertullian (*On Prayer* 13) recognizes the prevalence of the custom and says that Christians defended it by quoting Matthew 27. 24; he, however, regards it as pointless. Compare Mark 7. 1-15.

2. Hippolytus doubtless does not think it necessary to prescribe attendance at the Sunday eucharists, assuming that no true believer would willingly absent himself. Regular weekday eucharists were not yet customary, although they were held at times of special prayer and fasting;[223] compare 25. 2. So the only weekday meetings he presupposes are gatherings for prayer and instruction according to the synagogue pattern. Evidently the emphasis was laid on instruction, with the Bible as textbook, and those who could read were expected to follow the passages cited. 1 and 2 Clement give an idea of the content and style of the teaching, which would be given by instructors like those of 16. 1.

3. On occasion local meetings were visited and addressed by teachers of higher rank, who are described in terms reminiscent of the New Testament prophets.

36

1. Complete manuscript Bibles were very expensive, and few lay Christians could have owned one. But portions of Scripture were within the reach of all.

2-3. Hippolytus follows Mark 15. 25, not John 19. 14, here. He deduces the hours of the Jewish ceremonies from his typology; no definite hour is prescribed in the Old Testament,[224] while in the Temple the morning sacrifice was offered before sunrise and the showbread was changed (on the Sabbath) still earlier. He cites John 10. 14; 6. 50.

4. Mark 15. 33. Hippolytus adds that the darkness came in answer to (Christ's[225]) prayer; possibly a conjecture of his own but more likely a "tradition".

5. At the ninth hour, as soon as Christ died, he went to the lower world and released the spirits in prison, who rejoiced with a great thanksgiving. The belief was very widespread[226] but the other versions seem to miss the point.

6. John 19. 34. The darkness from the sixth to the ninth hour, followed by daylight until evening, made a "night" and a "day"; so the Son of Man by Easter morning had truly been "three days and three nights in the heart of the earth" (Matthew 12. 40). Compare Constitutions V, 14. 9-13.

9. On the custom of rising during the night for prayer, compare, e.g., Tertullian, *To his Wife* II, 5. Hippolytus—rather more than Tertullian—insists that unbelievers should not witness Christian devotions.

10. John 13. 10 repeals the provisions of Leviticus 15. 16-18.

11. Despite the principle just enunciated Hippolytus cannot rid himself of a belief that a purification is needed; he compromises by declaring that a small ceremony will suffice. Compare chapter 37.

12. This quaint doctrine—which the other versions omit or alter—came from the authorities who gave Hippolytus the rest of his "tradition". He mentions them here only, but in Irenaeus similar appeals to "the presbyters" are numerous.

13. Matthew 25. 6, 13 in an unusual text form.

14. Peter's denial (Matthew 26. 74) is synchronized with the condemnation of Christ by the Sanhedrin.

37

The sign of the cross is performed after first breathing on the hand, so that it is wet with saliva. Belief in the power of spittle to repel evil spirits is widespread[227] and, despite Hippolytus's disclaimer, lies behind the practice he advocates. His own interpretation of the ceremony is none the less ingenious; the mixture of moisture and breath[228] corresponds to the water and the Spirit in baptism and so makes the sign of the cross the "image" of baptism, accomplishing a sort of rebaptism[229] (36. 11). Only Latin A has the original; Latin B and the other versions do not understand the custom and replace "baptism" by "the Word".

The interpretation of Exodus 12. 22 is in the style of Barnabas.

38

CONCLUSION

Hippolytus closes with a final adjuration to avoid all novelties; the way of peace consists solely in strict adherence to the past.

FOOTNOTES

[1]Luke 12. 13-16.

[2]For exceptions see, e.g., Romans 14. 14 (= Matthew 15. 11), 1 Corinthians 7. 10 (= Matthew 19. 9), 1 Clement 46. 8 (= Matthew 18. 6, in substance), 2 Clement 12. 2 (apocryphal).

[3]Especially in 2 Clement.

[4]Acts 15. 28-29.

[5]Romans 14, in particular.

[6]1 Corinthians 8. 8; 10. 25-26.

[7]Compare Revelation 2. 14, 20.

[8]Didache 13. 7, etc.

[9]Didache 13. 3, etc.

[10]So very emphatically in 1 Clement 40-41. But Clement does not argue for a detailed parallelism between the two ministries.

[11]Didache 3. 1-6 is an instance.

[12]The reason for this appears to be that at this period the Fourth Commandment was conceived to be wholly

"ceremonial", and to "keep the Sabbath" was regarded as Judaizing (Ignatius, *Magnesians* 9. 1, etc.). The belief that in Christianity the Sabbath laws have been transferred to Sunday is of medieval origin.

[13]On these methods compare especially K. E. Kirk, *The Vision of God* (London, 1931), pp. 119-124.

[14]As in Wisdom 14. 25-26.

[15]Romans 1. 29-31 is largely of Greek origin; 1 Timothy 3. 2-3 and Titus 3. 1-2 are wholly so.

[16]In 1 Clement 47. 6 the forty-five year old Corinthian church is called "ancient".

[17]Jude 17, Revelation 21. 14, etc. The meaning in Ephesians 2. 20 is probably a little different.

[18]1 Clement 42. 4; 44. 1-2, etc.

[19]Even in the third century liturgical prayers were still normally extempore, and use of a fixed form was regarded as a weakness on the part of the officiant.

[20]Eusebius, *HE*, v, 24.

[21]See especially James Muilenburg, *The Literary Relations of the Epistle of Barnabas and the Teaching of the Twelve Apostles*, Marburg, 1929.

[22]39th Festal Letter (367), 7.

[23]The details of the Patristic testimony are best seen in J. R. Harris, *The Teaching of the Apostles*, Baltimore and London, 1887.

[24]*Die Didache*, Bonn; many editions.

[25]*Didascalia Apostolorum*, Oxford, 1929.

[26]Also known as Third Clement. Occasionally—and unfortunately—called the Apostolic Canons or the Roman Church Order.

[27]Paderborn, 1914. Dr Schermann's theory of a very early date for the document is individualistic.

[28]Pp. 127-138, 233-244, 295-306.

[29]Often reprinted separately.

[30]But incorrectly.

[31]Pp. 34, 78, 40.

[32]Cooper and Maclean, p. 18.

[33]*HE*, VI, 20.

[34]*Vir. ill.* 61.

[35]His festival is on August 13.

[36]Not completely legible; reproductions are not always to be trusted.

[37]*Origenis Philosophumena*, Oxford. Books II-III are presumably still missing, although it has been argued that what is ordinarily called Book IV may contain them; Wendland, however, rejects this theory (p. xvi).

[38]Especially in his *Hippolytus and Callistus*, 1853.

[39]*St Clement of Rome*, II, pp. 317-477. First published in 1869; in the later editions the argument is slightly expanded but is otherwise unchanged.

[40]Jerome, *Vir. ill.* 61.

[41]Legge (II, p. 127) unfortunately revives Döllinger's remarkable explanation of this occurrence: Callistus had lent the bank's funds to the Jews and went to the synagogue to recover his depositors' money. As if anyone would expect Jews to transact business on the Sabbath and at a synagogue service!

[42]Victor's accession occurred about 189, and Commodus died in 192.

[43]The distinction between "martyr" and "confessor" was not yet developed.

[44]Or perhaps restored the privileges of the office to him; when and where Callistus was ordained is uncertain. Possibly he had the confessor's ordination (p. 39).

[45]Hippolytus's account of his controversy with Callistus is, in fact, so bitter that modern historians feel obliged to interpret it in the sense that will make the greatest allowance for the latter. Hence less than full justice is perhaps done nowadays to Hippolytus.

[46]The antithesis "In time or in eternity?" seems hardly to have been stated squarely until the beginnings of the Arian controversy.

[47]And Zephyrinus?

[48]Less probably after Zephyrinus's death.

[49]Hebrews 6. 4-8, 10. 26-31, 12. 17.

[50]Except, perhaps, through martyrdom.

[51]Matthew 13. 30.

[52]Romans 14. 4.

[53]His most violent treatise—the Philosophumena—was perhaps omitted, but time has so defaced the list that we cannot be certain. The Apostolic Tradition, however, was duly listed, and it certainly contains polemic enough.

[54]*Theologische Literaturzeitung*, 1920, col. 225.

[55]Compare the Epitomist's "The Constitutions of the Holy Apostles through Hippolytus".

[56]London.

[57]Leipzig (*Texte und Untersuchungen*, VI, 4).

[58]Hippolytus's work is printed on pp. 101-121; reprinted in Connolly (pp. 175 ff.), and in part in the fifth edition of Duchesne's *Christian Worship*, London, 1919.

[59]II, pp. 97-119.

[60]The notes are systematized and amplified in the latter's *Ancient Church Orders.*

[61]*Unbekannte Fragmente altchristlichen Gemeindeordnungen*, Berlin Academy.

[62]*Über die pseudoapostolischen Kirchenordnungen*, Strassburg.

[63]Facsimiles in Hauler.

[64]Compare p. 60.

[65]The oldest (Sahidic) is dated *ca.* 1005.

[66]Details in Horner.

[67]More logical and so secondary.

[68]This seems easier than Schwartz's theory (p. 7) of a *later* Sahidic text enlarged from the original Greek.

[69]The former cautiously.

[70]It lacks chapter 6.

[71]Epitome 4.

[72]Possibly "in those places"; so Horner interprets the Ethiopic.

[73]And Ethiopic. The Greek has "through thy beloved Son Jesus Christ thou gavest to thy holy apostles".

[74]So the Greek, not the Latin.

[75]Latin and Ethiopic (MSS), "Father, who knowest the heart"; perhaps better.

[76]Not in the Epitome but in the Latin, Ethiopic, Constitutions, Testament and Canons.

[77]The doxologies suffer probably more than any other phrases by transmission. The translation given follows no text precisely but represents what seems to be the most likely original form.

[78]The indicative, "ye perform", of the Latin is a misrendering of the (ambiguous) original Greek.

[79]On the doxology compare note on 3. 7.

[80]The Latin might also be rendered "Not with ordinary words but with similar power". But the Ethiopic confirms the above translation.

[81]Literally "Cause that from thy sweetness there may not recede this fruit of the olive".

[82]An Ethiopic section (Statute 5) generally printed here (7) is not by Hippolytus; compare pp. 30-31.

[83]Reading "presbyteri" for "presbyteris".

[84]Testament "in holiness to thy holy place"; Ethiopic "in thy holy of holies".

[85]Testament "from the inheritance of thy high-priesthood".

[86]Testament adds "and purely and holily".

[87]Testament "high and exalted office". The Ethiopic manuscripts differ considerably in their renderings of "he may ... office"; Horner's *a* reads "having served the degrees of ordination he may obtain the exalted priesthood". But only *a* reads "priesthood".

[88]Doxology conformed to preceding; that in the Testament is rather different.

[89]With the Sahidic agree almost exactly the Arabic, the Testament and the Canons. The Ethiopic has been edited from a different view point.

[90]These words seem clearly implied by the context; Hippolytus has now concluded the discussion of ordinations proper.

[91]Ethiopic and Arabic omit this "not", making the passage senseless.

[92]The Ethiopic makes the sense of the original clear.

[93]In the Sahidic the readers and subdeacons precede the widows.

[94]So the Ethiopic and Arabic. Sahidic reads "nor does she conduct *liturgia*".

[95]Compare last note.

[96]Epitome 13.

[97]The Sahidic misjoins "new" with "faith".

[98]The Ethiopic adds "or if a woman has a husband".

[99]Following the variant Sahidic reading in Horner, p. 436.

[100]The Constitutions show that the Sahidic is right against the other evidence ("let his master's permission be gained").

[101]The Constitutions (32. 3) have preserved the original here, which the Sahidic renders freely.

[102]The Sahidic, against the other evidence, adds "according to the law".

[103]The Sahidic amplifies.

[104]Supplied to give the obvious sense.

[105]The Ethiopic shows that this is the sense; the Sahidic has misunderstood the use of "authority".

[106]Literally “nor cause him to swear”.

[107]“Male harlot”?

[108]This Sahidic list has been interpreted from the list in Constitutions 32. 11.

[109]So the Sahidic and the Testament. The Ethiopic and Arabic have “shall exact an oath from each one of them”.

[110]Obscure, but apparently original. The Ethiopic and Arabic have “for it is not possible for an alien to be baptized”; the Testament “for the vile and alien spirit abides in him”.

[111]Sahidic “and”.

[112]Supplied for clarity.

[113]The Sahidic and Ethiopic have “to the bishop or presbyter”; the Arabic has “to the bishop”.

[114]Or the sense may be that the presbyter, the candidate and the deacon all stand naked in the water; in the above translation “the candidates” was supplied for “them” and the following “them” was substituted for “him”.

In the Sahidic, Ethiopic and Arabic the deacon causes the candidate to repeat a rather elaborate creed: the Sahidic form is: “I believe in the only true God, the Father Almighty, and His only-begotten Son, Jesus Christ our Lord and Saviour, and in [the] Holy Ghost, the life-giver to the universe, the Trinity in one substance, one Godhead, one Lordship, one Kingdom, one faith, one baptism in the Catholic apostolic holy church. Amen”.

The Canons agree practically with the Testament.

[115]This question is omitted in the Sahidic, Ethiopic and Arabic, but it is found in the Canons.

[116]The Canons add at this point: 'Every time he says at the baptism: "I baptize thee in the name of the Father and of the Son and of [the] Holy Ghost, the Trinity in unity"'. None of the other sources have anything corresponding.

[117]Jungklaus includes this paragraph in the preceding chapter.

[118]Here the doxology is given as it stands in the Latin. But compare the earlier doxologies.

[119]The Latin adds "In Greek *antitypum*".

[120]The Latin adds "In Greek *similitudinem*".

[121]Evidently omitted by accident.

[122]Vienna fragment.

[123]An Ethiopic section generally printed here (24) is not in the other versions and is irrelevant to the context; it will be found on p. 58.

[124]The apparent sense.

[125]Or, "this bread is 'blessed bread'; it is not 'the bread of the thanksgiving', as is the Body of the Lord". The Sahidic translator probably did not understand the original Greek exactly.

[126]The Latin adds, "What in Greek is called an *apoforetum*".

[127]The apparent sense.

[128]Literally "make haste".

[129]Literally "make the blessing".

[130]Sahidic "that we all should be sober and that the heathen may envy us". The Ethiopic adds a long section that has no parallel in other sources; see p. 58.

[131]Literally, "on account of the lot that falls". Perhaps: "because of his (their?) duties"?

[132]Friday, Saturday and Sunday after midnight.

[133]So the Latin and the Testament. The Sahidic, Ethiopic and Arabic have "before the proper time to eat".

[134]The texts have "when he has learned the truth"; the above, however, seems to be the meaning.

[135]31-32 are omitted here; they will be found on p. 60.

[136]Literally "let everyone choose for himself to go to that place".

[137]Sahidic "for".

[138]The apparent sense.

[139]Literally "be the last".

[140]Literally "things thou thinkest not".

[141]Literally "breaks forth"; the Latin (31. 3) has "blooms".

[142]Interpreting the Sahidic ("that thou mayest know how") by the Testament ("that is like to").

[143]Interpreting the ambiguous Latin with the Sahidic.

[144]Latin B, which is followed by the Oriental versions, is translated above. Latin A (compare p. 60) reads: "But seek always modestly to sign thy forehead; for this sign of his Passion is manifested against the devil if it be made from faith; not as pleasing men, but knowingly offering it as a breastplate. For the adversary, seeing the power of the spirit coming from the heart in the publicly formed image of baptism, is put to flight, thou not yielding, but breathing at him. And this was that [sign formed] when Moses, as a type, put the blood of the lamb slain at the Passover on the lintel and anointed the two side-posts, signifying the faith which now we have in the perfect Lamb".

[145]Latin B and the Oriental versions have "the Word". But "baptism" is needed for the sense.

[146]In chapter 38 the two Latin texts are in virtual agreement.

[147]A gesture of respect.

[148]Literally "the sealing". Perhaps all food sent to the sick is meant; but the passage is far from clear.

[149]Literally "count".

[150]The apparent sense.

[151]The Ethiopic manuscripts vary in the form of the doxology.

[152]In Ethiopic use the Hallelujah Psalms are 104-106, 134-135, 145-150.

[153]Compare 26. 5-6.

[154]The restoration of sections 30-31 is conjectural.

[155]In this last sentence the (unintelligible) Latin has been corrected by the Sahidic.

[156]P. 35.

[157]Although not in discarding chapters 33-34 also.

[158]Pp. 77-83.

[159]See below.

[160]Acts 20. 28, etc.

[161]Romans 12. 1, 1 Peter 2. 5.

[162]Hebrews 13. 15, Revelation 8. 3.

[163]Philippians 4. 18, Hebrews 13. 16.

[164]1 Corinthians 11. 21.

[165]Compare p. 68.

[166]Many editions and translations; the best in English is A. L. Williams' edition in the S.P.C.K. series of *Translations of Ancient Documents*, London, 1921.

[167]Genesis 1. 31.

[168]1 Timothy 4. 4-5.

[169]Ignatius, *Smyrnaeans* 7. 1, etc., and Didache 9. 1, 5, are the earliest instances.

[170]It should be needless to remark that this recital of the institution is merely part of the historical narrative, and is wholly devoid of other implications. It was in no way thought necessary for the rite; compare the Didache and for later liturgies see, e.g., Cooper and Maclean, pp. 170-172.

[171]1 Corinthians 10. 3, John 6. 63.

[172]IV, 18, 4-5; I, 13, 2. Incidentally, Irenaeus teaches an invocation of the Logos, not the Spirit.

[173]1 Clement 44. 4, Didache 15. 1.

[174]Possibly a copyist's error, misreading "facietis". The Greek was of course ποιεῖτε.

[175]Through its use in St James it supplied the model for the Scottish and American Prayer Books.

[176]Mark 6. 13, James 5. 14.

[177]Compare Constitutions VIII, 30.

[178]Compare *ibid.*, 29.

[179]The search for Greek antecedents has not been fruitful.

[180]English edition by H. Danby (S.P.C.K., 1919).

[181]πρεσβυτέριον or συνέδριον; the latter word passed into Aramaic as *sanhedrin.*

[182]In Jerusalem, however, the high priest presided as the religious head of Israel.

[183]In Judaism priesthood came by birth, not by ordination. The office had little dignity.

[184]A Rabbi's authority was that of his personal learning. Very few presbyters could have been Rabbis, except in Jerusalem.

[185]The temple worship entered little into the outlook of most Jews. Outside the temple priests had almost no functions.

[186]"Adjuvet et gubernet"; in Greek (Constitutions VIII, 16, 4, Epitome VI, 2) ἀντιλαμβάνεσθαι καὶ κυβερνᾶν.

[187]Certain meals held by religious societies of Jews were only a specialized form of family devotions.

[188]Didache 15. 1.

[189]Best studied in the Didascalia.

[190]In very large churches conditions were different.

[191]Possibly implied in Constitutions VIII, 46, however.

[192]Most explicitly in Horner's *a*.

[193]In Hermas "martyrs" (the word used) includes confessors. The Vision, of course, purports to describe a scene in heaven, but it naturally reflects the earthly status.

[194]In Rome *ca.* 250 there were only forty-six presbyters (Eusebius VI, 43, 11); evidently confessors were not included.

[195]E.g., Eusebius VI, 43, 6, where confessorship is called "the highest honour".

[196]Yet the fact that the section goes on to threaten confessors who made clerical claims shows a different tradition existed.

[197]Eusebius VI, 43, 11.

[198]Eusebius, *l.c.* The other minor orders were doorkeepers, readers and acolytes. All are still extant in the Roman Catholic church, although now only as stages through which candidates for the priesthood pass; the same is virtually true of the subdiaconate and diaconate also.

[199]Acts 2. 41, 8. 38, 16. 33.

[200]In this passage "he sighed" should be rendered "he breathed".

[201]Compare Justin, *Dialogue* 116 f.

[202]Compare Sarapion.

[203]Leviticus 15. 5, etc.

[204]Contrast the reading of the Canons given in 19. 18.

[205]The trine formula in Matthew 28. 19 is textually insecure.

[206]Epistle 70 (69). 2.

[207]1 Corinthians 12. 13, etc., John 3. 5.

[208]Popular Christian terminology was not so hesitant.

[209]Baptism.

[210]Exodus 3. 8, etc.

[211]But the Testament has no words of administration for the wine.

[212]Due, presumably, to combining this section with the preceding. The Canons add eternal life and the eucharist.

[213]E.g., Constitutions VII, 45, 1. Compare the position of the Prayer in the Didache.

[214]Mark 6. 30-44; 8. 1-10 and parallels.

[215]Compare 1 Corinthians 11. 20-21.

[216]*Romans* 7. 3; compare *Smyrnaeans* 7. 1. In *Smyrnaeans* 8. 1-2 the words are perhaps distinguished.

[217]1 Corinthians 11. 20.

[218]Since the benedictions used over eucharistic bread and wine and agape bread and wine (if wine was to be had) may have been identical, early Christians may often have been in doubt as to the meaning of a meal.

[219]P. 68.

[220]Literally "steadfast".

[221]Riedel misses the meaning of *ksms.*

[222]Compare Tertullian, *On Prayer* 18-19 for exaggerations of the same thought.

[223]The "stations" of Tertullian, *On Prayer* 19.

[224]Exodus 29. 39; 25. 30.

[225]So explicitly in the Ethiopic.

[226]1 Peter 3. 19.

[227]E.g., Galatians 4. 14.

[228]Impurity can also be blown away; compare 20. 8 and (e.g.) Tertullian (*l.c.*).

[229]Connolly (p. 104) prefers to say that the ceremony "is in some sense an integral part of the one and original baptism".